JOSEPH L. KISH, JR., is Corporate Records Manager, Olin Mathieson Chemical Corporation. He has contributed scores of articles to business journals and is a Contributing Editor of *Systems* magazine and Consultant to *Computers & Data Processing* magazine. Mr. Kish also lectures for the American Management Association and is a member of the Association of Records Executives and Administrators and the National Microfilm Association. In addition, he conducts a course on microfilm information storage and retrieval systems at New York University.

JAMES MORRIS, an editor with the Edison Electric Institute, was formerly editor of *Systems* magazine. Mr. Morris has written widely on photographic equipment, data processing, and other business and industrial subjects, and is co-author (with Joseph Kish) of *Paperwork Management in Transition* published by the American Management Association.

MICROFILM
IN
BUSINESS

JOSEPH L. KISH, JR.
OLIN MATHIESON CHEMICAL CORPORATION

JAMES MORRIS
EDISON ELECTRIC INSTITUTE

THE RONALD PRESS COMPANY · NEW YORK

Foreword

All too familiar are the mountains of records and vast libraries of information needed for present-day business, industrial, and engineering operations. Automatic data processing systems offer help in indexing such information, but current machine languages are pathetically inadequate as a storage medium for illustrations or lengthy documents.

To be useful, much of today's basic documented intelligence simply must be retained in its original form. Microfilm makes such retention manageable. It can compress data in a ratio of 99 to 1 compared with original bulk—while retaining the vital capability of returning the original in the form of a true paper replica. In addition, as brought out in this book, the overall control of microfilm records is usually simple and relatively inexpensive compared with the complex equipment needed for automatic data processing. Simple manual indexes suffice in most cases to control microfilm files. However, well-conceived microfilm information retrieval systems with indexes that are searched by automatic data processing equipment have proved most valuable in large-scale business, institutional, and government operations.

While the improper and uninformed use of microfilm can act as a positive barrier rather than an aid to efficient document control and retrieval, when used intelligently, microfilm can become a prime tool for business operations both large and small. The busy executive plagued by the fact that he is more and more frequently unable to locate information he urgently needs would be well advised to investigate an appropriate microfilm system. The businessman who wants only to organize and secure the monumental stacks of dusty records that must legally be kept indefinitely can also profit by taking a good, hard look at microfilm. For such studies, this book is invaluable.

Microfilm in Business presents a logical, non-technical approach to the concepts of microfilm systems. It neatly fills an important need for those interested in learning the facts of business microfilming.

RICHARD W. BATCHELDER
President, Graphic Microfilm Corporation
Past President, National Microfilm Association

Preface

This book is designed to answer many questions about the use of microfilm in recording business operations and for records storage. Many records managers have regarded microfilm primarily as a means of "dead storage" for documents rarely referred to, but whose retention is necessary for legal or other reasons. However, the new systems technology has developed useful microfilm applications in retrieving and controlling the active records used in day-to-day business that can be of even greater importance. These applications are carefully examined in the course of this book.

The various types of microfilm, such as roll microfilm, aperture cards, and microfiche, are examined as systems tools, with indications of where each is likely to be most useful. The book also points out those situations where microfilming may not be advantageous in setting up an effective and economical information and storage system. It shows how to analyze costs and determine whether a system is practical and economical in a given situation and how independent microfilming services may be used in conjunction with internal operations.

In addition to suggesting efficient approaches to deciding what kind of microfilm should be used for retaining financial and sales records, research references, engineering drawings, and other types of information, the book discusses methods of filming and appropriately indexing documents. The linking of microfilm files

with automatic data processing equipment for information retrieval, the permanency of microfilm, and the legality of microfilmed records are also discussed. Explanations and diagrams
provide a basic understanding of the differences among various
types of photographic stock and the working principles of cameras,
processors, and printing and enlarging equipment.

For their help in obtaining and evaluating material for this
book, we would like to thank the following: Neil McKay and
Jim Scanlan of the 3M Corporation, Richard Maslyn and Fred
Sauter of the Recordak Corporation, Robert Rudolph of Graphic
Microfilm Corporation, Rodd Excelbert of *Systems* magazine, and
Belden Menkus of the Kennecott Copper Corporation.

Joseph L. Kish, Jr.
James Morris

New York, New York
  January, 1966

Contents

APPENDIXES

MICROFILM
IN
BUSINESS

Chapter 1

Why Microfilm?

Microfilm is simply another systems tool like punched paper tape and the tabulating card. Like any other systems tool, microfilm has its place in a company's overall information program. Properly utilized, it can solve problems; in the wrong application, it can *create bottlenecks and cause needless expense.* This book will try to aid the records manager by noting applications where the use of microfilm is likely to be impractical or costly, as well as the multitude of applications where it can solve difficult paperwork problems.

There are generally five reasons why a company should want to preserve records on microfilm rather than in some other way:

1. Conservation of space and equipment
2. Vital records protection
3. An information storage and retrieval tool
4. As part of an active business procedure or system
5. To facilitate reproduction or transmittal of records

It is worthwhile to note that three of the five reasons given involve day-to-day active business systems rather than storage. It is not wise or profitable to consider microfilm merely as a tool for saving space. In fact, it is sometimes overused in that particular application. Let us consider one by one these five general applications of microfilm as a business systems tool.

CONSERVATION OF SPACE

Many companies initially use microfilm in an effort to reduce the number of file cabinets, the volume of filing supplies, and the amount of floor space required to hold the filing cabinets. Microfilming is quite effective in reducing the volume of records. In fact, microfilmed records will usually occupy only 2 per cent of the space taken by records in their original form.

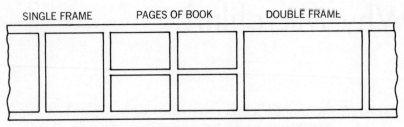

SINGLE FRAME   PAGES OF BOOK   DOUBLE FRAME

35mm ROLL MICROFILM AND COMMON PROPORTIONS
OF IMAGE IMPOSITION

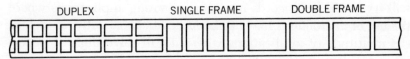

DUPLEX   SINGLE FRAME   DOUBLE FRAME

16mm ROLL MICROFILM AND COMMON PROPORTIONS
OF IMAGE IMPOSITION INCLUDING DUPLEX

Fig. 1–1. Sizes of roll microfilm images.

As can be seen in Fig. 1–1, there is a wide variety of image sizes available on standard 16mm and 35mm roll microfilm to suit the nature and size of original documents to be recorded. At bottom left are tiny duplex flow camera reductions of about 40 to 1. These are commonly used by banks in recording both the back and front of canceled checks. At upper right is the much larger double-frame 35mm image employed in microfilm aperture cards used to contain engineering drawings. If an original document, such as a large drawing, needs still more microfilm image area, the drawing can be divided into sections and recorded on two or more double-frame images. Much larger 105mm microfilm is also used in certain specialized applications.

There is a danger, however, in arbitrarily relying on microfilm as the only means of reducing the costs involved in the storage of extensive and bulky records. With today's improved records management techniques, it is generally possible to store records in their original form in a low-cost records storage area for eight years or more before the cost of storage equals the cost of microfilming. Therefore, careful analysis should be made before it is decided to microfilm any records for space or equipment savings *alone*. This problem will be explored in detail in Chapter 5.

With the above qualification, microfilm is obviously well adapted to the long-term storage of original documents. However, in a modern business, original documents are by no means the only type of records that make excessive demands on space. For instance, another area in which microfilm is proving effective in cutting costs and freeing costly equipment for other purposes is in the mechanized data processing area. As more and more business procedures are programmed for computer processing, the greater a company's outlay will be for tabulating cards, magnetic tapes, and special filing equipment. Canceled punched card checks, for instance, may be more economically preserved on roll microfilm for legal purposes than by storage in their original form.

Management is becoming more aware of microfilm's capability as an alternate information storage and retrieval device. A company can reduce its data processing cost by printing out and then microfilming records stored on tab cards or tape. We are referring here to records that will not be required for use in further computations, but which nevertheless must be retained for tax, legal, research, or historical purposes. Such records would actually be more accessible on microfilm.

It is very often desirable to microfilm files of records that include charts and graphics as an essential part of the documents (laboratory notebooks, for example) and records that require authentication for validity, such as leases and contracts. The physical storage of such records is often a clumsy process, since they often do not fit snugly in standard files. Reducing them to machine language for storage in an automatic data processing system is usually impractical. Yet many companies are not sufficiently aware of the simple but effective microfilm indexing systems that can make such material readily retrievable while its bulk is reduced to a fraction of its former size.

PROTECTING VITAL RECORDS

The second common reason for deciding to use microfilm is to protect vital records against loss through disaster, theft, or negligence. Many of the largest companies in America now use microfilm as a means of assuring the security of essential information. There are two important advantages in using microfilm for vital records protection.

1. Since many documents can be stored on a single roll, they generally will not present a space or storage problem.
2. In many instances, it is more economical to duplicate a large volume of records by making a duplicate roll of microfilm than by using another copying process, such as an electrostatic office copier.

But we must inject some words of caution at this point. Frequently, vital information may already be protected by being available in two or more distant locations. This is generally true of financial and sales data. The expense of further protection by microfilming may be unnecessary.

Then, too, when deciding on microfilm for vital records protection, it is necessary to remember that reproduction equipment will be needed to blow the microfilm images back to readable size. In case of a national disaster, for instance, microfilmed records locked in a cave would be of little immediate value unless the cave also contained operable reproduction equipment. Most such repositories now provide this equipment.

INFORMATION RETRIEVAL

Indexing systems for microfilm files start with simple target and flash card techniques. They include methods such as the relatively simple Recordak "Lodestar" system of identifying microfilm images by means of code lines printed on the microfilm along with the document. They also include extremely complex indexing systems where immense files are cross-indexed and can be automatically searched with the aid of the computer. There are information retrieval systems utilizing microfilm to fill the needs of almost any size or type of business.

AS PART OF PROCEDURE

Frequently, microfilm is used as part of a standard business procedure. For example, many banks microfilm their customers' checks prior to returning them with the bank statement. Most large department stores return original sales receipts charged by customers against their accounts with a copy of the customer's monthly statement. Before doing so, however, the stores will microfilm the charge slips to obtain a copy for future reference.

FACILITATING REPRODUCTION

Finally, microfilm is used to facilitate reference reproduction and transmission of documents. As an example, a company's engineering department may decide to microfilm original tracings, since the microfilm is obviously easier to handle than the large, many-sized tracings. Another example would be that of a company required to forward copies of research material from one location to another. A good system for handling this problem might be to microfilm the documents and transmit them to the requesting location. There, a high-speed microfilm electrostatic printer (the Xerox Copyflo, for example) could supply any number of hard copies for local use.

Generally, the decision to use microfilm will be based on two or more of the five factors described here. A manufacturer, for instance, might decide to microfilm his tool drawings to (1) save space, (2) provide more records protection by making a duplicate copy at the time of filming, and (3) facilitate reference reproduction, since duplicate drawings could be readily available at remote locations.

The important thing to remember in using microfilm or any other systems tool is that you must carefully examine your needs to obtain benefits in terms of efficiency and savings. Whatever information storage and retrieval tool you use to solve a particular problem, be sure that it is the one best suited to that application.

HISTORICAL DEVELOPMENT

How did our modern microfilm business systems develop? The concept of microfilm is almost as old as the technique of photography itself. In the 1850's, not long after Daguerre's development of the photographic process, experimenters began to make microphotographs at reduction ratios as great as 150 to 1. Such microphotographs later attracted attention when imitated commercially and mounted at the end of small magnifying tubes that made it possible to read souvenir messages on tiny chips of film.

Microfilm had its first important application during the Franco-Prussian War. With Paris under siege, the surest way out of the French capital was by air. A surprising amount of traffic managed to move out of the city in free balloons. Unfortunately, it was not feasible for the balloons to return. The city was a tiny target for a drifting balloon, and the prevailing winds were not helpful.

French photographic technicians attacked the problem and managed to institute an efficient airmail service between Paris and Bordeaux with the aid of carrier pigeons and microfilm. Their pigeons, carrying almost weightless rolls of thin film sheets in their tails, succeeded in flying out of range of Prussian shotguns and mostly evading the Prussian falcons sent up to stop them.

But it was not until after World War I that ways were found to solve important business problems with microfilm. The innovation that opened the way was the development of the rotary microfilm camera by George McCarthy, a New York City bank clerk and amateur inventor of modest means whose outlook was in the tradition of the great American inventors.

McCarthy frequently encountered problems on his job when customers claimed that their account had been debited for checks never drawn. Since the bank returned canceled checks to its customers, it frequently was not possible to determine whether the customer was telling the truth. So McCarthy set out to invent a machine that would make a photographic record at high speed of all checks deposited. With the aid of an engineer partner, he worked out a machine in which a check conveyor belt was synchronized with a motion picture camera. They applied for a patent in 1925.

The device was big and clumsy and had plenty of "bugs." Checks on some colored papers did not photograph clearly, for instance, and neither did signatures in light blue ink. While bankers showed interest in the check photographing machine, they were not interested enough to purchase it. The engineer partner grew discouraged and McCarthy bought him out.

Shortly afterward, McCarthy's resolution paid off in storybook fashion. The management of Eastman Kodak Company had also learned about the machine, and they showed more than just interest. Kodak signed a handsome contract with McCarthy involving a lump sum payment, future salary, and royalties. Then Kodak put its engineers to work ironing out the kinks in the check recording machine. Good progress was made and, by 1933, there were 700 machines operating in American banks. The machine had, by then, been given the name Recordak.

Active commercial use of microfilm in the control of business records outside the banking field was also promoted by the new Recordak Corporation in the 1930's. Rotary cameras went into use for such purposes as making records of retail receipts in department stores. Stores adopted systems whereby they mailed sales receipts to customers as proof of purchase after making a microfilm record, thus saving considerable extra paper work.

Companies were also learning to reduce the physical volume of old but not "dead" records by putting them through a rotary camera and storing them on roll microfilm. In addition, librarians were using film to make expendable records of valuable documents for public use. They also began to use film to provide easy-to-handle copies of clumsy records such as newspaper files.

In World War II, microfilm made possible a tremendous worldwide airmail operation. To speed what would have been impossibly heavy loads of airmail to millions of troops overseas, messages were photographed on long rolls of 16mm film by rotary cameras. Only the rolls of microfilm were shipped by air, to be printed out as hard copy on the once-familiar V-Mail envelope near the end of the journey. High-speed, continuous enlargers performed this job. V-Mail made microfilm a household word.

Also during World War II, the development of a simple but very important record-keeping device, the microfilm aperture card, brought microfilm sudden additional importance. The aperture card, as well as being a convenient means of compressing bulky files of engineering drawings, is a method of linking the data holding capacity of microfilm with the speed of automatic data processing equipment. At both government and industrial engineering facilities, the aperture card proved a convenient answer to the problem of storing and referring to tremendous amounts of engineering data. The words "referring to" have even greater importance than the word "storing." Hard copies of full-size engineering drawings in block-long rows of pigeonhole files were often of limited usefulness because of the physical effort required to maintain and search them.

The success of the aperture card called attention to the fact that efficient microfilm retrieval systems need not be complicated. Although the aperture card is composed of a chip of microfilm fixed to a punched card designed for automatic sorting, it was found that, in the average engineering drafting department, automatic sorting was rarely needed. The cards could be manually retrieved from an ordinary file.

It was also frequently discovered at this time that records on roll microfilm could be retrieved, checked, and duplicated quite easily. The compact microfilm reader-printer, introduced in the 1950's, made the use of microfilm in active office applications a much more convenient matter.

Now in the 1960's, microfilm techniques are being merged to an even greater degree with electronic data processing. Systems that permit the calculations of computers to be recorded directly on microfilm in the form of graphs and charts, rather than in machine language on magnetic tape, are being put into use. The microfilm *image* is often being found a more compact storage medium than electronic impulses on tape. Equipment manufactured by General Dynamics Corporation, for instance, uses a cathode ray tube as a computer output to project graphic images on microfilm. Another method of storing computer output on microfilm is used by the U.S. government's giant FOSDIC data processing system and is mentioned in Chapter 7.

Experimental equipment that might be said to almost completely merge the techniques of magnetic recording and microfilming has also been demonstrated. The General Electric

Company has shown a microfilm technique called thermoplastic recording that bypasses the chemical development of images recorded on standard light-sensitive film and uses instead a method of electronically imposing and fixing an image on the film.

This radical approach is, in its basics, not too complicated. The film has two coatings that take the place of the light-sensitive emulsion on the type of microfilm we are familiar with. One coating (the one underneath) will absorb and hold a tiny electronic charge. The coating over it is sensitive to heat and will become molten if its temperature is raised to a certain point. When the film is heated, the electronic charges impressed upon the inner coating have a physical effect on the outer coating, causing it to ripple slightly. With heat removed, this outer coating hardens in a fraction of a second, and a permanent record, in the form of a microscopic ripple pattern, is left on the film. If the electronic impulses on the inner film represent an image, the permanent record on the outer layer of film will also represent an image.

The ripples function as tiny lenses. When projected on a screen, the diffraction pattern of the projected light forms an image that can be sensed by the eye. Color as well as black-and-white images can be obtained in such a projection process. The image on the film may also be erased, so that the film can be used many times over.

Probably, thermoplastic recording is only one of many developments to come that will increase the importance of microfilming as an information and communications tool.

Chapter 2

Microforms

The microfilm industry has long recognized a need to develop new and varied ways of preparing and filing microfilm to meet the requirements of different applications. Today, microfilm is available in many forms, ranging from roll film to film chips. In addition, either positive or negative images can be provided to suit the needs of a system.

The form in which microfilm is prepared is called a *microform*. The National Microfilm Association defines microform as "a generic term for any form, either film or paper, which contains microimages."

The term "unitized" as used here will refer to microforms that are planned as one complete unit or subdivision of information without reference or attachment to any unrelated or extraneous material. Examples of unitized microforms would include microfiche and microfilm jackets. Roll microfilm, on the other hand, usually contains a variety of unrelated information units on the same roll. It would therefore be referred to as a "non-unitized" microform.

The various microforms now widely available for use in records management are the following.

ROLL FILM

This is the most common microform. Documents are filmed in 100- or 200-foot lengths and, after processing, are filed away on reels. Roll film may be either positive or negative. When viewed, negative film provides a white image on a black background, while positive film provides a black image on a white background.

Negative film is ideally suited for the rapid, inexpensive production of enlarged copies of microimages as well as the reproduction of additional positive copies of the microfilm roll. Many people prefer positive roll film for direct viewing, since they find the black-on-white images more natural and easier on the eyes than the white-on-black image available from negative film.

One large company's technical library uses both positive and negative roll film in their operation. Periodically, they microfilm their copies of technical reports and memoranda. After processing, the negative microfilm is used to reproduce a positive microfilm roll. The negative roll is then shipped to an off-site facility for vital records protection purposes, where it will be available in the event all other copies of the technical reports and memoranda are destroyed or lost. The positive microfilm roll is used in the technical library for reference purposes.

The use of roll microfilm has one clumsy aspect. That involves the updating of files already microfilmed. If you desire to unitize such files, you will have to splice microfilms of all additional related documents received into the original roll. This is a slow and laborious process.

UNITIZED MICROFILM

If you wish to unitize a particular group of microfilm records, you will probably want to use one of the following systems: (1) microtapes, (2) acetate film jackets, (3) microfiche, (4) micro-opaque cards (more commonly known by the trade-name "Micro-cards"), or (5) microfilm aperture cards.

Two of these systems, microtape and acetate film jackets, have actual add-on capabilities and are therefore ideally suited for applications in which unitized files must be updated. Microfiche and micro-opaque cards, however, have no add-on capability. They are best suited for applications in which a unit of information is complete at the time of filming, and no further updating is required after the unit record is made.

Microtapes

Microtapes are prepared as a continuous printing operation. Negative roll microfilm is used to prepare a positive microfilm image of 16mm or 35mm photographic paper tape with pressure-sensitive adhesive backing. After processing, the microtape is simply cut to the proper length and pressure-applied to ordinary index cards.

Microtapes possess excellent add-on capabilities, since any particular microtape card may be updated without refilming an entire group of documents. However, additional copies cannot be prepared from microtapes, so that a person wishing to refer to a particular document at his work station must borrow the entire card. Consequently, there is the possibility that the borrowed card may be lost or damaged while out of file. Also, requests for it may come in while it is away on loan. These are the principal disadvantages of microtape.

Microtape systems have proven valuable for one company's Industrial Medicine Department. Faced with a limited amount of office space in which to contain expanding medical facilities and the records of a constantly increasing number of employees, this department microfilmed each employee's medical file. Positive microtapes were prepared from each of these negatives and were mounted on standard 5" × 8" index cards—one per employee. These cards were then filed alphabetically in a standard card file. Any reference required to a medical file may be quickly made by using a microfilm reader capable of reading positive microimages. The difficulty of making full-scale reproductions of the images prepared on microtape is not a factor in this application, since the records are for Industrial Medicine's use only and copies are rarely required.

As new records are generated for each employee, they are batch filed, alphabetically by employee name. Monthly, all new records are microfilmed, and again positive microtape copies are prepared. These are then added to the appropriate employee's microtape index card. As before, the original records are destroyed.

This system has reduced the amount of space required for Industrial Medicine's files, speeded up reference to these files, and reduced the possibility of misfiled documents.

Acetate Film Jackets

If a unitized microform possessing both add-on and reproduction capabilities is required, the acetate film jacket should be considered. These jackets are made in standard index card sizes ($3'' \times 5''$, $4'' \times 6''$, $5'' \times 8''$, etc.) of clear acetate. Each is commonly separated into pockets (called chambers) by paper dividers glued between two sheets of acetate. Into these chambers can be inserted short strips of microfilm. The transparency of the jackets permits reproduction of enlarged copies of any micro-image filed in the jacket on a suitable reader-printer without removing the film from the jacket.

Acetate jackets provided an efficient, economical solution to a pharmaceutical manufacturer's record-keeping problems recently. This manufacturer, as part of its research operations, annually awarded a large number of medical grants to doctors, hospitals, dentists, etc., for the field testing of its products. The reports returned by each grantee became a significant portion of this manufacturer's research files and were scheduled for a twenty-year retention period.

As the number of products grew, so too did the number of grantee reports on file. Soon, a major record-keeping problem faced this manufacturer—there was no more space in which to store these reports, and reference to them was unnecessarily slow and inaccurate.

For a solution to this problem, the manufacturer turned to microfilm. However, since files would be continually updated, roll film would be impractical. Likewise, Microtapes would prove unsatisfactory, since enlarged reproductions of the microfilmed records would be frequently required. Therefore, a system was developed providing for each grantee's file to be microfilmed in roll form. The rolls would then be cut, and the strip containing each grantee's reports would be inserted into an acetate jacket, clearly labeled with the grantee's name. The original records would then be destroyed, while the microfilms, mounted in acetate jackets, would be retained for future reference.

When reference was required, the appropriate jacket was simply inserted into a microfilm reader-printer, capable of accepting acetate jackets, and enlarged to readable size. When reproductions were required, they were quickly obtained at the push of a button.

Newly received reports were batch filed by name of grantee and periodically microfilmed. The originals were then destroyed and the processed microfilm cut and inserted into the appropriate acetate jackets.

This system has been in use for over a year and has proven satisfactory.

Microfiche

Microfiche is a newly popular unitized microform that groups together related microimages on a clear transparent acetate card. The image is printed on this single sheet of acetate. This microform is discussed in detail in Chapter 4. It has a number of advantages when used for both distribution and duplication of technical reports and is being widely adopted at U.S. government agencies.

Micro-Opaque Cards

Micro-opaque cards are similar to microfiche but contain a positive image on paper cards. Documents are photographically reproduced as unitized groups of positive microimages in a grid pattern on a white card. The result resembles a page of a calendar. These cards may be printed on either side. Individual microimages may be enlarged and viewed on a microfilm reader-printer capable of accepting them. Normally, these cards are used only in applications where direct viewing is required, since reproduction, while not impossible, is slow and costly when contrasted with the easily reproducible negative microfiche image.

A major use of micro-opaque cards is for the miniaturization of bulky, expensive technical periodicals, such as the *Patent Gazette* and *Chemical Abstracts*. Many companies find it more economical and convenient to subscribe to such publications reproduced in micro-opaque form than in the original hard-copy form.

Aperture Cards

In certain applications, particularly the processing of engineering drawings, it is most convenient to unitize a microfilm record by mounting it in a standard tabulating card. This very important system is described in detail in Chapter 3.

Film Chips

Certain microfilm information retrieval systems, such as Mini-card and MEDIA, utilize microfilm that has been cut into small sections or chips for automatic or semiautomatic storage and retrieval. Generally, particular sizes of film chips have little or no application apart from the system and equipment for which they were designed. They are discussed more fully in Chapter 7.

Chapter 3

The Microfilm Aperture Card

An aperture card is a standard EAM (electric accounting machine) key-punch card in which a rectangular hole has been cut (Fig. 3–1). A microfilm image is mounted in such a way as to cover this hole or aperture. Such a card can be inserted and examined in most microfilm readers. The image (usually a reduction of a large engineering drawing) can be blown up in a printer to provide readable hard copy. The card can be stored in a small fraction of the space that is required to hold the original drawing. If the aperture card is key-punched, it can, along with thousands of other such cards, be quickly sorted by EAM equipment. Of course, few companies actually sort aperture cards by machine because they are so readily accessible in file drawers. Also, for machine sorting, strict standards must be observed with regard to adjustment of the sorting machines and mounting of the microfilm. But there are situations, in government and large manufacturing firms in such fields as aerospace, where machine sorting is indispensable to complex information retrieval requirements.

Microfilm aperture card systems were thought at first as being best adapted to giant operations. The experience of recent years has shown this to be most untrue. Smaller companies with engineering departments totaling twenty to twenty-five people have

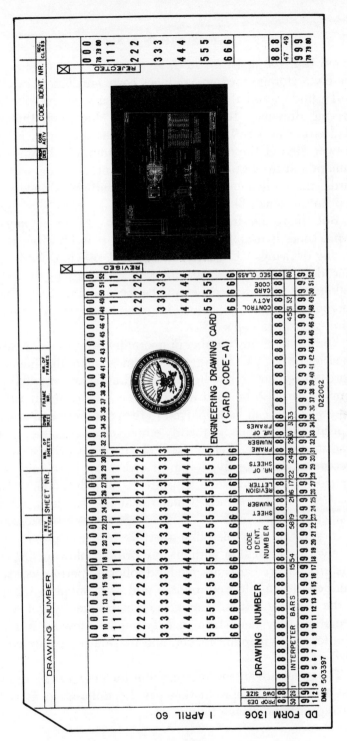

Fig. 3-1. Microfilm aperture card.

19

found that the aperture card, as an active systems tool and not merely a storage medium, reduces costs and increases efficiency.

To understand this, it is only necessary to examine an engineering drawing. It is a large clumsy document that must be filed either as a roll in a pigeonhole file case, or in a large, flat drawer file. If these drawings are photographed by a planetary camera and the resulting microfilm mounted in compact aperture cards, the equivalent of thousands of full-size drawings can be kept in one small file drawer.

But this is far from the whole story. In an engineering file room, there is usually much activity in searching for and reproducing drawings. Engineers must check previous work and combine design elements from different drawings in the process of making revisions and developing new designs. Reproduction of microfilmed drawings is much faster and more simple than making a full-size diazo copy.

For instance, any number of microfilm printers can easily reproduce an 18″ × 24″ enlargement from a microfilm image that is more convenient to handle than the draftsman's original product. Printers can also be used to produce a duplicating master of the same size that can be employed to turn out any number of copies. A printer of this type frequently employed in engineering drawing repositories is the "Xerox 1824" electrostatic printer, which can accommodate a steady stream of orders for checking prints. In typical installations, such a printer is usually employed in conjunction with the standard diazo printers that turn out full-size duplicates of drawings.

In addition, the microfilm aperture card can provide an engineer with information without any printed blowup. At the time master aperture cards are made, duplicate aperture cards can be produced in any desired number and distributed to satellite files in the drafting rooms. Engineers can frequently get all the information they need from a drawing by viewing it for a few minutes on a microfilm reader, and make a print only when they need it.

The great advantage of microfilm for engineering drawings is that the kind of reproduction can be tailored to *fit the need*, cutting cost and saving time.

Another important advantage is the control microfilm gives the chief engineer and the systems analyst over the accuracy of the information used by engineers and draftsmen. In the past, when copies took longer to make, engineers tended to set up personal files relating to the designs they most often dealt with. A copy of a drawing filed away near an engineer's desk or drawing board could go through a number of revisions unknown to him. Really serious losses could take place if he used an outmoded drawing as the basis of a design. With engineering departments having swelled in size in so many companies and depending on enormous amounts of reference material, such confusion can easily occur without tight controls.

Microfilm is a tool in preventing this confusion. So long as the engineer knows that information is readily available from an up-to-date master aperture card file, or from a satellite file near his desk, without the prospect of painfully waiting for it, he is much less likely to bother with dubious personal files of material that may be outmoded.

The filing and distribution of engineering drawings has been a longstanding problem that was aggravated in recent years by the great expansion of engineering and design activity. There has always been a lack of uniformity in the size of original engineering drawings. They can range anywhere from $8\frac{1}{2}'' \times 11''$ to $36'' \times 48''$ under normal circumstances. In the past, their reproduction depended entirely on the comparatively slow speeds of diazo equipment.

Thus, a company was faced with one of two unsatisfactory alternatives in handling their distribution: (1) reproduce more copies than were needed to make them generally available, or (2) slowly reproduce drawings as requested. The first alternative led to an increase in space and reproduction costs; and, since additional reproductions might never be used because of obsolescence or low demand, this often proved expensive. The second alternative led to an increase in costly waiting time by high-salaried technical help.

An aperture card system can change all this. Briefly, such a system calls for the microfilming of new and revised engineering drawings, and the subsequent mounting of individual microimages in a standard 80-column tabulating card. If desired, these cards may be key-punched (indexed) to describe necessary data. The aperture card takes up part of the 80-column key-punched area, but there is adequate space remaining to include considerable information, such as the drawing number, project number, and revision date. A key-punched aperture card can be automatically sorted in standard tabulating equipment as well as manually. However, potential users should be cautioned that some automatic data processing equipment must be modified so that the microfilm area of the cards will not be damaged when sorted by machine.

These aperture cards, being of uniform size, can be stored in standard tabulating card file cabinets. When copies of a particular drawing are requested, the request may be answered in one of two ways:

1. By preparing an enlarged (up to 18″ × 24″) print by means of a microfilm printer
2. By preparing a duplicate aperture card

In either instance, the time and cost involved in answering the request are low compared to that of reproducing a full-size print of the original drawing.

PLANNING A SYSTEM

Each company's needs are different in detail. Initiation of a feasibility study and careful planning are therefore important to the success of any aperture card microfilm program. Failure to consider all needs may result in a needlessly expensive or inappropriate system.

Before embarking on a microfilm engineering drawing system, obtain the answers to the following questions:

1. Is a microfilm system for engineering drawings economically feasible?
2. From a practical standpoint, is it the best system for your company?
3. Does opposition exist that would make it unwise to consider such a system?

Although this is not so true today, opposition was once common when department personnel discovered that microfilming requires fairly strict standards for the quality and cleanliness of drawings.

To obtain the answers to these questions, the following information should be obtained:

1. Which departments currently use engineering drawings, or similar material, at the location under study?
2. For each of these departments, determine the number of professional people, the number of clerical people, the physical location of their offices, and the type of work performed.
3. Do the professional people need to carry drawings away from the office?
4. What systems and equipment for filing and reproducing engineering drawings does each of these departments use?
5. What types and sizes of drawings does each department have (original tracings, blue lines, white prints, etc.)? What is the quantity by department?
6. What percentage of these drawings are active or current?
7. How are reproductions now made for each department? How many are made each day by each department?
8. Are the engineering drawings self-generated, or are they received from an outside source? If received from an outside source, are they prints, tracings, or both?
9. What is the daily average of new drawings? Revised drawings?
10. Have people in the departments involved been exposed to, or worked with, a microfilm system for drawings? Are there any predetermined feelings about such a system?

As this information is obtained, we suggest you tabulate it in a manner similar to that shown in Fig. 3–2. If it appears that there is little or no resistance to be met, it is suggested that you proceed directly to building up a cost comparison between the present method of producing full-size prints and the proposed aperture card system.

In the unlikely event that there is resistance, the records manager may find it advisable to meet with the various dissenting parties and try to convince them of the importance of taking a fresh, open-minded view of the proposed system. In most such cases, it is only necessary to explain the dollars-and-cents value of

	Ammunition Research	*Ammunition Development*	*Design Engineering*
Number of departments	3	6	3
Location	Bldg. 61	Bldg. 61	Bldgs. 114, 983
Number of professionals	22	16	41
Need to carry drawings away?	Yes	Yes	Yes
How are repros. made?	Xerox Photostat Photocopy	Ozalid White print	Ozalid
How filed?	Tubes Files	Files	Files
Type drawing used	Ozalid White print Original Blue line	White print Ozalid Blue line Original	White print Ozalid Original
Size drawings	8½″ × 11″ to 30″ × 36″	8½″ × 11″ 22″ × 34″	8½″ × 11″ to 36″ × 48″
Quantity	15,000	42,000	75,000
How many active?	10%	90%	90%
How many reproductions made daily (average)?	15	165	364
Self-generated	50%	90%	85%
Received from outside	50%	10%	15%
What form received from outside?	Prints Tracings	Prints	Prints Tracings
Any preconceived opinions?	No	No	Yes—in favor of microfilm

Fig. 3–2. Tabulation of results of systems study.

microfilm and other obvious advantages over the present system. Once you have agreement, you are in a position to proceed with your cost analysis. The following is suggested:

Finding Present Costs

1. Annual costs of reproduction paper and supplies. You can get this from the previous twelve months' invoice for reproduction paper and chemicals. Normally, this will also require developing a percentage figure for the number of engineering drawings reproduced compared with the total number of all reproductions.
2. Estimated annual labor cost for reproduction personnel producing prints. Again, this will require apportionment of a percentage of total salaries.

3. Estimated annual labor cost for files personnel expenditure.
4. Value of floor space occupied by engineering drawings files and vaults as well as the space occupied by reproduction equipment.
5. Value of non-productive time spent waiting for prints. For this figure, estimate the percentage of print requests not filled because the drawings were not available in the files (already in use, lost, misfiled). The best way to determine this percentage is to take a representative sampling over a period of one or two weeks. Then apply the following formulas:
    a) Total requests per month multiplied by the percentage of out-of-file prints equals total prints missing per month.
    b) Total of prints missing when requested multiplied by average number minutes required to obtain print equals minutes required per month waiting for out-of-file prints.
    c) Minutes required per month divided by 60 and multiplied by average hourly salary multiplied by 12 equals annual value of non-productive time.

Adding these five subtotals together will give you the cost of your present system. Then you are ready to go on and find the cost to your company of a microfilm system for handling engineering drawings.

Cost of Aperture Cards

1. Annual cost of master and duplicate aperture cards and blowups can be found as follows:
    a) Total new and revised drawings made monthly (count two drawings for any that are 36″ × 48″ or larger) multiplied by maximum cost per film-mounted aperture card equals total monthly master aperture card cost.
    b) Average number of copies of each new or revised print prepared multiplied by number of new or revised drawings issued monthly multiplied by maximum cost of duplicate aperture card equals monthly cost for duplicate aperture cards.
    c) Total monthly master aperture card cost plus total monthly duplicate aperture card cost multiplied by 12 equals annual cost for master and duplicate aperture cards.
2. Annual cost of film can be found as follows:
    Number of drawings issued or revised monthly divided by 550 equals number of microfilm rolls required. (Note: Al-

ways count each drawing 36″ × 48″ or larger as two drawings.)

3. Annual cost of duplicate aperture cards requested *after* initial
   distribution must also be determined as follows:
   Estimated number of new or revised drawings requested
   monthly after initial distribution multiplied by maximum cost
   of duplicate aperture card multiplied by 12 equals annual cost
   of duplicate aperture cards required after initial distribution.

4. Estimate labor costs next. Normally, two persons are needed
   to key-punch the aperture cards and mount the film in them.
   However, there are automatic processor-cameras that produce
   fully processed aperture cards in less than a minute. These
   units are of desk-top type and are best adapted to situations
   where just a few drawings at a time are to be put on microfilm
   aperture cards (see Chapter 10).

   a) Total annual salary of microfilm personnel divided by per-
       centage of time spent in microfilming engineering drawings
       equals annual labor cost for microfilming engineering draw-
       ings.

   b) Total number of new or revised aperture cards issued an-
       nually plus total number of duplicate aperture cards issued
       annually multiplied by five minutes equals maximum time
       spent in filing, refiling, and returning aperture cards annu-
       ally. Maximum time spent filing, refiling, and retrieving
       aperture cards multiplied by average hourly wage equals
       annual labor costs for files personnel. Average filing time is
       something that can vary from installation to installation.
       The maximum figure of five minutes suggested here must be
       judged against the records manager's experience.

   c) Annual labor cost for microfilming personnel plus annual
       labor cost for files personnel equals total annual labor cost.

5. Next, compute the annual value of floor space saved. Generally,
   a microfilm engineering drawing system will occupy one-tenth
   the floor space of systems using full-size originals and copies.
   Using the floor space determined for your present system's cost,
   determine this figure.

6. Value of non-productive time while prints are out of file does
   not have to be computed since the master aperture card is never
   loaned out and is immediately refiled after reference.

Adding these totals together gives you the cost of the proposed
microfilm engineering drawing system. You can now determine

the estimated savings to be realized by conversion to a microfilm system.

Survey of Drawing Methods

Once it appears that economy and convenience will result from the conversion to an aperture card engineering drawing system, it is essential that a fairly detailed review be made of current drawing practices as well as the condition of current drawings to determine whether they will reproduce properly on microfilm.

First, spot-check drawings that would be included in your system. Are they in good condition? Is a good contrast provided between the lines of the drawings and the material it is drawn on? Are many drawings dirty or smudged? Are there many erasures on the drawings? If any of these conditions are present, the microfilming of these particular drawings may prove unsatisfactory. If these conditions are prevalent in the majority of drawings, it may be necessary to limit your system to newly created drawings only.

Next, review drawing practices in your engineering department. Start with the type and size of the lettering used. Is it large enough to reproduce a legible image when viewed on a microfilm reader, or reproduced on the reader-printer?

Drawing quality may require upgrading. Since erasures will generally reproduce on microfilm, it will be necessary to tighten standards and request the department head to reject as unacceptable drawings with excessive erasures.

Is color coding used to any great extent? If so, you will be faced with the choice of using color microfilm or noting on the drawing what the color is and where it is. Under most circumstances, color microfilm will be found impractical because of high cost, delayed processing, and lack of image sharpness.

It might also be necessary, if such is not your company's practice, to standardize the use of drawing pens and pencils, the thickness of lines, the use of typewriter ribbons, the positioning of rubber stamps, and the adding of reference marks to the drawing to insure consistently good results when engineering drawings are put before the camera.

The above covers most of the changes that may be required in your company's drawing practices. Others may become apparent, but these include most of the common problems for which you should be alert.

Naturally, resistance may arise to some of these changes; but, if you point out that these changes also constitute a move toward good drawing procedures, you should be able to overcome such objections. You should also point out that an efficient microfilm system will reduce delays, thereby speeding production. Engineers and draftsmen will understand the importance of this.

INSTALLING THE SYSTEM

You should now be in a fairly good position to make a proposal to management concerning the installation of an aperture card engineering drawing system. The only question is: At what point should you begin? Should you recommend that the system include only current or active drawings, and that obsolete and inactive drawings be retained in their original form? If possible, and especially if space is a problem, it is most desirable to include all possible drawings in the compact microfilm system. However, other factors must be considered. The older drawings may not be good enough in too many cases to produce usable microfilm images. Tests are necessary to determine this. Also, inactive drawings are infrequently referred to, so there would be no advantage in ease of referral, but only in saving of space and greater security. Frequently, it is advisable to limit an aperture card system to active drawings only, but sometimes microfilming of older drawings is necessary to preserve the information on them. When justified, special photographic processes can be used to improve the clarity of faded drawings.

Unsatisfactory Drawings

It is recommended that any drawing that is not clearly reproducible be retained in its original form. For such a drawing, an aperture card can be prepared containing only a microfilm target stating that, due to the unsatisfactory condition of the original drawing, it has not been microfilmed, and that any reference should be to the original copy. The target would note the location.

Filming

It is recommended that your microfilm camera be set up as close to the area in which the drawings are maintained as possible. Following the plan outlined in Chapter 6, someone familiar with the drawings should assist the camera operator in his work. Some firms program their conversion to microfilm when plants are shut down for vacation, so as not to disrupt production.

Filming is done with a standard planetary camera equipped with a pull-down device that automatically advances the film a sufficient distance after each exposure to provide for a mounting surface at the edges.

Use of 35mm film is standard, unless for some special requirement it may be necessary to use 70mm or 105mm film. Because of the high reduction ratio, 16mm film is unsuitable for practically all engineering drawing applications.

As each drawing is filmed, its number should be noted on the Microfilm Index, as described in Chapter 6.

Image Quality

Resolution and density are two factors that determine the quality of a microfilm image. Resolution obtainable with camera and film system is determined by viewing a filmed test target through a microscope and determining the number of lines per millimeter that can be visually discerned. Density is measured by a special apparatus called a densitometer. This device is used in evaluting a microimage to determine whether or not it was correctly exposed. Normally, the acceptable range for background density is between 1.0 and 1.2.

It is necessary if you must submit copies of your mcirofilm to any agencies of the Department of Defense to have a competent technician determine the resolution and density of your microfilm. The fairly complex Department of Defense Specifications for microfilm quality are covered in Appendix B.

Aperture Card Coding

Before actual filming has begun, you should have worked out an indexing system (see Fig. 3–3). Consider the type information about each drawing you will need to include on an aperture card. Certainly, you will want to include the drawing number and revision date. In addition, you might find it advisable to record such information as original drawing size, stock numbers of parts described in the drawing, project number, and other data. Depending on how elaborate your system is, this information may be typed on the aperture card, or it may be both typed and key-punched.

CARD COLUMN

1-10 Drawing Number	11-24 Reference Drawing	25-29 Project Number	30-31 Sheet Number	32-35 Revision Number	36-41 Revision Date	43-44 Security Class
C643200000	0000097410	1126	01	0000	120364	U
B000077890	3642988362	0084	03	0007	041962	S
H974112100	RSP757863	2700	02	0012	060164	C

Fig. 3–3. Example of key-punch indexing systems for aperture cards.

Although aperture cards are designed to be key-punched for automatic retrieval, the cards are removed manually from files in order to fill day-to-day requests for one or more duplicates or prints. Automatic searching and sorting of aperture card files is likely to occur infrequently and mostly in large-scale operations, but it is done very frequently in such places as large missile plants. There is usually no real need to key-punch aperture cards when a modest file is initially set up, but many smaller firms do this from the outset in anticipation of expansion. Whenever the time comes, you will need to draw on the experience of your company's data processing department, and perhaps also obtain assistance from the sales technicians employed by data processing and microfilm equipment manufacturers.

Mounting

To facilitate this operation, the microfilm and the tabulating cards need to be arranged in the same order. This will be the case if the drawings listed on the key-punch work sheet are in the same order as the microfilm listed on the Microfilm Index.

Reproduction and Distribution

After the microfilm images have been mounted, they are ready for reproduction and distribution to the various print cribs requiring them. Duplicate aperture cards can be prepared by using a card-to-card printer (described in Chapter 10). After these duplicates have been prepared, the master aperture cards are immediately refiled.

Filing

Because the aperture cards are a standard size, no special filing equipment is required to store them. They may be conveniently and safely stored in standard tabulating card file cabinets. To facilitate reference, each aperture card should be interpreted and filed in drawing number order. Whenever reference is required, or a master aperture card is removed to prepare duplicate copies, care should be taken to assure that it is promptly refiled after use.

For maximum economy, it is generally advisable to "batch" the drawings to be reproduced. This will reduce non-productive walking time. One large aeronautics company has found that, by processing all requests for duplicate copies of aperture cards once every half-hour, they have been able to make maximum use of personnel and equipment.

Processing Revisions

In instances where a drawing is scheduled for revision, the appropriate aperture cards should be clearly marked to that effect. One way is to use a tab or a stamp reading:

THIS DRAWING IS BEING REVISED

BY   DATE

Then, if a request comes in for copies of this drawing, the requester simply checks with the person preparing the revision to learn what the changes are. At some companies, aperture cards are destroyed upon being superseded; at others, they are retained and form a master file of drawing changes. Depending upon your company's application, you will have to determine which approach you will take.

Chapter 4

Microfiche

Microfiche is a newly popular form of microfilm in which a related group of images are arranged on a card-shaped transparent sheet of film in the same way that the days of the month appear on a calendar. See Fig. 4–1.

The great value of the microfiche is that all the pages of a report or handbook can be contained in a convenient unit easy to handle in a microfilm reader or printer and easy to duplicate for distribution. It represents a very simple information handling concept that can be readily understood.

CHARACTERISTICS AND USES

Although the microfiche has been used abroad since the beginning of the century, it found little acceptance in the United States until recently. The most extensive early use of this form of microfilm was in the libraries of a few European countries, principally France. However, the growing need for a "unitized microform," a medium for recording and reproducing in one convenient unit *related groups of images,* led to another look at microfiche by American technical libraries and information specialists charged with difficult projects.

Such government agencies as the Atomic Energy Commission and the National Aeronautics and Space Administration turned to microfiche in the last few years to solve their growing problems

in indexing and distributing the vast amount of technical information required by research laboratories and government contractors. It is easy to see why they became interested. The microfiche satisfies a need that cannot usually be filled by devices such
as the now-familiar aperture card in the distribution of technical information. While the aperture card provides an excellent
medium for storing, sorting, indexing, and retrieving engineering
drawings, there are limits to the amount of information that can
be placed on one aperture card.

Sometimes, a number of cards have to be used to hold the
microfilm image of one large engineering drawing. When parts
of the same information unit will be separated in handling, it
naturally makes for reduced efficiency and convenience. This
happens only infrequently in the case of drawings, but with
technical reports and manuals, the situation is usually different.
Making fifty or more aperture cards to hold the pages of a detailed report would be a clumsy operation, and the results would
be more difficult to mail and distribute than a microfiche.

However, records managers at companies with active aperture
card programs will find that the aperture card can substitute for
the microfiche in holding technical reports—provided these reports
are fairly brief. It is possible to get about eight average-size
pages of text on a microfilm image suited to mounting in an
aperture card. If the facilities are already there, this may be the
most simple and economical systems approach—until length and
volume of reports increase.

There is also another microfilm medium for distributing lengthy
units of information. In some handbook and specification sheet
operations, for instance, microfilm cartridges containing short
strips of roll microfilm have been used to hold government specifications to contractors. This system predates the current interest
in microfiche among defense agencies and contractors, but it does
not offer the same advantages in handling, distribution, and duplication of information.

Also, even though the microfiche has received little publicity
in the United States until recently, a variation of the standard
microfiche known as a micro-opaque card or "Microcard" (trade-
mark of the Microcard Corporation) has been employed in this
country for over ten years to reduce a long list of magazines and

Micro Photo Microfiche

Sample Microfiche Showing
Miscellaneous Varied Size Material

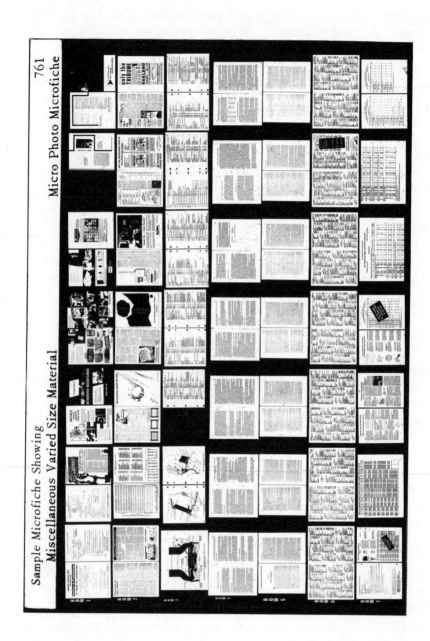

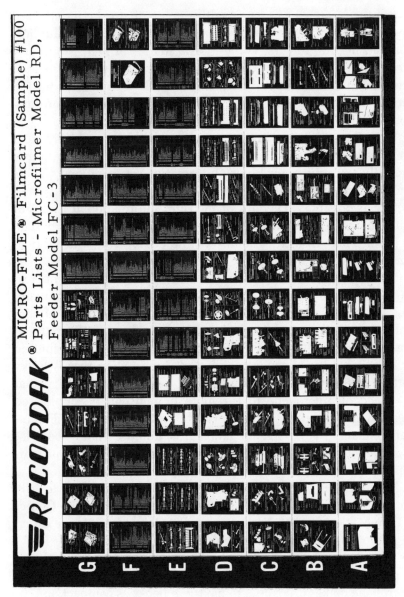

Fig. 4–1. Two microfiche transparencies. The top is positive, the bottom negative.

35

scholarly publications to a simple paper card varying in size from
3″ × 5″ to 6″ × 9″.

But the Microcard bears a positive image that is better adapted
to reading in a viewer than to requirements that call for duplication and making full-size copies. As a matter of fact, the Microcard Corporation expanded its activities in recent years to include
standard microfiche operations, and it acts as a contractor for the
Atomic Energy Commission in that agency's microfiche information program.

With the paper-work and information problems resulting from
the missile race, the government found itself operating a number
a rapidly expanding new library-information organizations. These
information dissemination centers have to do their jobs as completely as possible. The lack of the right information at the right
time can mean extremely expensive delays in a research program,
or it can mean disastrous failure in the engineering and fabrica-
tion of a missile.

Many jobs for microfiche are now being found in a number of
business areas outside the government-agency-contractor network
where the paper-work explosion has also been getting out of control. Companies, particularly large organizations with scattered
branches, are finding microfiche a handy medium for distributing
reports, procedures manuals, and other information that is bulky
and expensive to duplicate and mail. A procedures manual that
is mailed on microfiche to a remote branch can be duplicated
there as required and easily stored for ready reference. For instance, mailing twenty microfiche cards would certainly be a lot
cheaper than mailing, say, the equivalent of 2,000 pages in hard-
copy form.

Microfiche is also well adapted to applications that primarily
involve long-term storage of information. At the Research Center
of Olin Mathieson, notebooks from research laboratories are stored
on microfiche for both research and legal purposes. These books
are usually 100 pages in length. They need to be indexed and
stored as is. There are no later additions to particular notebooks.
Microfiche makes it possible to file these books as compact and in-
divisible units. Legally, this has the advantages of relating a
particular piece of research or development work to a particular
time and place.

One of the first commercial uses of microfiche in the United States was begun a few years ago by the publishers of the *Thomas' Register*. Instead of a shelf of thick directories, the company is now able to offer customers a compact 4″ × 6″ card file containing the same information. Also, this is an application where use of microfiche makes it easier to update the *complete file* of information by substituting new units. Where previously it would have been necessary to wait for a new edition to incorporate new information into a directory, additional microfiche cards containing the latest information can be easily added.

Many businessmen are familiar with a very common type of microfilm medium that often looks like a microfiche but is not. This is roll microfilm cut and stored in transparent jackets. These jackets are often approximately the same size as a microfiche card, but their application is different. Here, strips and chips of microfilm containing one or more documents can be added and subtracted manually to update the information in the jacket—something that cannot be done with microfiche. Such an arrangement is obviously well adapted to many applications where copies of deeds, wills, school or hospital records, and many other documents need to be stored in *flexible* units that can be altered as necessary. There would rarely be a requirement to distribute or reproduce all the information in a jacket in this type of file.

Wherever lengthy records must be saved as a unit, and referred to and duplicated, microfiche can be a great convenience. In applications where the same information unit must be altered or added to frequently, the jacket is more useful.

SPECIFICATIONS

Microfiche systems reduce a document to anywhere from 1/18th to 1/24th its original size. Other reduction ratios may be used, but an effort is currently being made by equipment manufacturers to develop standards that would confine reduction ratios between 1:18 and 1:24.

Either of the two types of microfilm camera can be used to make microfiche. The common office-type rotary camera that photographs documents as they move along a conveyor belt produces roll microfilm that can be cut into appropriate lengths, coated with adhesive backing, and stripped onto a transparent microfiche film card. The result is a microfiche negative. When a planetary camera (one in which the document is photographed while stationary on a bed) is used, roll microfilm is also produced, and the procedure is the same. However, in many government and service company facilities, microfiche are prepared by special planetary cameras with step-and-repeat film units. These cameras are so constructed that they can register the film images in a gridiron pattern on a rectangular sheet of film. When this sheet of film is developed, it is a microfiche negative and the stripping process is bypassed.

Microfiche cards may be prepared in any size. However, most current users employ one of the following: $3'' \times 5''$, $4'' \times 6''$, $5'' \times 8''$, and tabulating card size. The application will generally determine the size card selected.

For example, at Olin Mathieson, it was necessary to use microfiche on a $5'' \times 8''$ transparent card to allow for the unitization of 100 filmed pages of a laboratory notebook microfilmed at a reduction ratio of 20:1. If the number of pages to be filmed were less, or the reduction ratio higher, it might have been possible to use a smaller card.

For ease of retrieval, it is necessary to provide a means of identifying one microfiche unit from another. There are two ways of making such identification possible with the naked eye:

1. Provide for the filming of a descriptive title on the first page of each document. This original title page should be at least $8\frac{1}{2}'' \times 11''$ in size with the words of the title each 2 inches high. The filmed result will be an index title that can be easily read with the naked eye.
2. Provide for the addition of a title block along the top of the microfiche card. This is a separate operation and usually involves the setting of the title by one of the cold-type processes and subsequent processing and stripping. Most microfilm service companies charge considerably more for the addition of such indexing.

The majority of microfilm readers and reader-printers now being marketed will accept microfiche for viewing and reproduction. It is, in fact, the overall ease with which reproductions can be made from microfiche that makes it such a convenient information storage medium. Inexpensive attachments are also available so that older readers and reader-printers can handle microfiche.

A duplicate microfiche may be easily and economically reproduced from a microfiche master by means of a card-to-card duplicator, and this reproduction will be comparable in quality with the original. If, however, it is decided to mass reproduce images contained on microfiche, the images may be enlarged on offset masters and then duplicated in large numbers. A positive opaque microfiche may also be prepared from the negative microfiche master if the application calls for a copy of microfiche document that will be used for reference purposes only.

Summing up, the advantages of microfiche over other types of microfilm can be stated as follows:

1. Microfiche provides a quick and economical means of preparing and distributing multipaged reports.
2. Because microfiche are unitized records of multipaged documents, they make possible the filing and easy retrieval of bulky material with a great reduction in filing space. Further, the reduction of all documents to a standard size eliminates the need for special filing equipment.
3. Most microfilm readers and reader-printers on the market will accept microfiche for viewing and reproduction. In addition, by means of a cutting and stripping operation, the output of any microfilm camera, either rotary or planetary, can be used to prepare microfiche. The result is lower conversion cost when the system is installed. A company can easily adapt its present equipment to a microfiche application.

In the event that in-depth indexing of a microfiche file is required, an additional index can be set up, either manually or with punched cards and computer. This will permit searching in a wide range of parameters when dealing with large files or complex material.

The microfiche is a record storage medium that is still more common to the scientist and librarian than it is to the businessman, but the increasing need to store and refer to complex unitized records—and to insure that record units are complete—makes the microfiche a tool worth examining.

Chapter 5

Job Cost Analysis

There are a number of reasons for a microfilming program in addition to the simple objective of reducing storage costs by eliminating bulky files. Whether a company's objective is a reduction in storage costs, a systems improvement, or both, it is still a normal and necessary procedure to determine the approximate costs before any microfilm job is scheduled. This cost figure should then be compared with the cost of maintaining the records in their original form in an inactive records storage area located in a commercial warehouse or on company premises.

Then, if the microfilm program should cost more than maintenance of the original records, it is possible to weigh this added cost against the value of systems improvements that may be obtained through a microfilm program. For instance, better reference and superior protection of vital records are two systems advantages that would have to be weighed against added costs—*if these should occur.*

As Figs. 5–1 and 5–2 show, the cost of microfilming the contents of a four-drawer file cabinet is approximately nine times the annual costs of storing these same records in a low-cost, inactive records center at a typical New York City location. It can also be argued that records are easier to read if stored in their original form, since the problem of providing microfilm readers and printers will not exist. On the other hand, it is equally true that

	Office Files	Records Center Containers	In-Plant Microfilming	Contractual Microfilming
Space required	6 square feet	1.7 square feet	Negligible	Negligible
Annual rental per square foot of floor space	$ 5.00	$2.45	Negligible	Negligible
Cost of required space	$30.00	$4.29	Negligible	Negligible
Filing equipment and supplies amortized	$12.00	$2.45	Negligible	Negligible
Record maintenance and overhead	$ 9.00	$2.55	Negligible	Negligible
Microfilming labor	None	None	$56.00 (4 days @ $14.00)	Built into contract price
Microfilm camera rental	None	None	$14.00 (4 days @ $3.50)	Built into contract price
Microfilm cost	None	None	$18.00 (4 rolls @ $4.50)	Built into contract price
Per image microfilm cost	None	None	None	Planetary . . . .$.04 Rotary . . . .$.015
Total cost	$51.00	$9.29	$88.00	Planetary . . . .$318.00 Rotary $122.00

Fig. 5–1. Costs of storing 8,000 documents in office files, records center containers, and on microfilm at a typical New York City location.

properly organized microfilm files can be much more easily scanned and examined on a microfilm reader than by searching through numerous dusty files of original documents. Which approach is best must be determined on the basis of predicted frequency of reference and the type of records involved.

However, it is still necessary to report, as is also shown in Figs. 5–1, 5–2, and 5–3, that modern records management techniques, utilizing low-cost storage areas, have reduced the costs of storing records in their original form to a point where this approach is generally cheaper than microfilming if records are retained in their original form for periods of less than twelve years. Only beyond that point will the cost of simple storage exceed that of microfilming. This is shown in Fig. 5–2 and depicted graphically in Fig. 5–3.

	Years Retained				
	1	*5*	*10*	*15*	*20*
Office files	$ 51.00	$255.00	$510.00	$765.00	$1,020.00
Records center containers	$ 9.29	$ 46.45	$ 92.90	$139.35	$ 185.80
In-plant microfilming	$ 88.00	$ 88.00	$ 88.00	$ 88.00	$ 88.00
Contractual microfilming	$122.00 to $318.00	$122.00 to $318.00	$122.00 to $318.00	$122.00 to $318.00	$ 122.00 to $ 318.00

↑
BREAK-EVEN POINT
(12 Years)

Fig. 5–2. Total cost of storing 8,000 documents in office files, records center containers, and on microfilm for varying numbers of years at a typical New York City location.

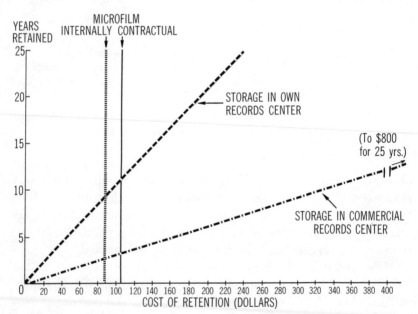

Fig. 5–3. Graphic comparison of costs of records retention methods.

Cost analysis is therefore a "must" before a microfilm program is undertaken. To obtain a meaningful picture of the situation, you will have to estimate costs in four ways:

1. Cost of on-premises microfilming, if you have the personnel to do this
2. Cost of microfilming your records at an outside service company
3. Cost of storing the original records on company premises
4. Cost of storing the records in a commercial warehouse

PROCEDURE

If you have determined the approximate number of documents to be filmed, you can estimate the amount and cost of the microfilm required by means of the following calculations:

1. Image per roll = $\dfrac{\text{Reduction ratio} \times \text{film length in inches}}{\text{Feed length of document} + 1}$

2. Rolls of microfilm required = $\dfrac{\text{Total documents to be filmed}}{\text{Images per roll}}$

3. Total price of microfilm = Rolls of microfilm required × microfilm price per roll + processing charge per roll

Next, estimate the amount of time required to film the documents under *ideal* conditions (no staples, all documents arranged in same direction, etc.). Add a 15 per cent fatigue factor to this to allow for operator fatigue, rest periods, and down time (time the machine is not in operation). Then consider the equipment you have available for the job. Will you have to rent a camera from an outside source? If so, be sure to include this charge in your analysis.

Estimate the labor involved in preparing the records for microfilming. This includes the effort needed in calling in documents from various locations, preparing them for filming, and indexing and redistributing them after filming. Multiply this time by your company's approximate clerical rate.

Next, estimate the amount of inspection time involved after the film is processed, as well as the amount of supervisory time you will spend on the job. Determine the costs of forwarding these microfilms for processing.

Finally, be sure to calculate the annual amortization or rental expense for any special equipment, such as readers and reader-printers that must be purchased or rented in connection with this microfilming plan.

An analysis must also include physical inspection of the records involved and an appraisal of the problems such records will present to the camera operator.

Although the various microfilm cameras are rated at 1,000 exposures or more per hour by the manufacturers, experience has indicated this figure to be excessive. It has been found that an experienced operator can be reasonably expected to average 750 letter-sized exposures per hour working with a rotary camera, and between 500 and 600 exposures per hour working with a planetary camera. But these speeds will not be attained if frequent exposure adjustments are required, if documents must be unstapled and restapled, or if documents are torn. So, at this point, it is advisable to review the documents against the Microfilm Checklist as follows:

MICROFILM CHECKLIST

1. Are records in good condition?
2. Are they free from staples and other fasteners?
3. Are they clearly legible?
4. Does good contrast exist between the recorded data and the color of the paper background?
5. Are they of similar size or color?
6. Are they free of significant data entries in color? The film will record color, but not as well as an entry in black.
7. Are the records complete—requiring no additional data or inter-filing—if a roll or microfiche system is to be used?
8. Are they free from frequent need for data comparison with each other?
9. Are they indexed simply and easily located under a numerical, alphabetical, chronological, or geographic system?
10. Will paper enlargements be required frequently?

A "No" answer to any of these questions is an indication that the job will be more expensive than normal. For example, if you find that 15 per cent of the documents to be filmed are of poor quality, you may feel that this will necessitate perhaps 10 per cent retakes, thus increasing your overall costs accordingly.

By adding the above cost factors together, you can determine the approximate total cost of microfilming the records under study.

THE MAKE-OR-BUY DECISION

If you decide to have the job done outside on a contract basis, reliable microfilm service companies will gladly provide you with estimates.

Be wary, though. Examine their detailed itemization of services offered in their bid price. Be sure, if they *do not provide* for such things as unstapling and restapling records, that you add the cost of your company's personnel performing this task to the microfilm service company's quotation. Also, be sure the microfilm service company agrees to follow your indexing system and that they agree to abide by the Department of Defense's specifications (if the records are to be used by an organization that requires them), and the American Standards Association's microfilm standards, or both.

STORING ORIGINAL RECORDS

The next step is to determine the costs involved in the storage of these same records in their original form in an inactive records storage area. First, let us consider storing them in a company-run area.

Company Storage Area

Initially, you will have to determine how many records storage boxes you will require. The easiest way to do this is to multiply the length of your records storage boxes by 100 (the approximate number of documents to an inch). This will indicate how many documents will fit in a single box. By dividing the total number of documents to be filed by the documents per box, you can quickly learn how many records storage boxes you will require.

Then by multiplying the number of boxes by the price per box, you will learn the total cost of these boxes.

Estimate the costs of preparing these records for storage by multiplying the estimated time required for packing, indexing, etc., by your company's average clerical rate.

Determine the amount of shelving space required to store these boxes. Then calculate one year's amortized value of this shelving.

Next, figure the square footage of floor space required to house all the boxes. Multiply this by the annual floor rental for a single square foot. The answer will be the total value of the floor space required.

Now determine the annual maintenance and overhead expense per box stored in your storage area by dividing the area's current annual operating cost by the total capacity of records stored. Multiply this by the number of boxes involved for the annual cost of maintenance and overhead for storing the records under study in the company storage area.

Add the following costs together: (1) maintenance and overhead, (2) floor space, and (3) shelving. Multiply this total by the retention period for the records under study (for example, 6.40×10 years $= 64.00). To this subtotal add the cost of the records storage boxes and the costs of preparing the records for transfer to storage. The total will be the cost of storing the records in a company-operated storage area for their total retention period.

Commercial Warehouses

If, however, your company does not have an adequate inactive records storage area on its premises, you should consider the use of a commercial warehouse, and contrast these storage costs with the cost of microfilming.

Again, determine the number of boxes required to store the records by multiplying the length of the box by 100. Then divide this answer into the total number of documents involved. The answer will indicate the number of boxes required. By multiplying this answer by the price per box, you will learn the cost of such boxes.

Now, estimate the amount of time required to prepare the records for transfer (packing of boxes, preparation of transmittal sheets, etc.). Multiply this time by your company's average clerical rate to determine the costs involved.

Determine the costs of transporting the records to storage as well as the warehouse's labor-in charge.

Next, multiply the total number of boxes to be stored by the warehouse's annual space charge. This will indicate the total annual rental for all boxes. Multiplying this figure by the number of years the records will be retained will give you the total warehouse rentals for those records.

Now add all these totals together. The answer will be the cost of storing the records under study in their original form in a commercial warehouse for their entire retention period.

By comparison of all three costs (microfilm, storage on company premises, storage in a commercial warehouse), you can determine easily which one is most economically feasible. Of course, as mentioned earlier, if other factors besides space and equipment savings are involved (better reference, vital records protection, etc.), these would have to be weighed against any cost differential.

The following examples illustrate how this cost analysis can be used to effectively determine the economic justification or lack of justification for microfilming records.

EXAMPLE OF WHEN **NOT** TO MICROFILM

Problem. A lumber dealer needs more file cabinets, file supplies, and floor space for the storage of current records. He is considering microfilming his Paid Accounts Receivable files. These files consist of approximately 45,000 $8\frac{1}{2}'' \times 11''$ documents, many of which are stapled. The records are mostly clear, readable carbon copies, and generally are in good condition. They are on white and light colored paper. These files are scheduled for an eight-year retention. After the first six months after payment, these files are seldom, if ever, referred to. (1) How much would it cost to microfilm these files? (2) Is this economically feasible, considering that these files can be stored in a nearby commercial warehouse for an annual charge of $1.50 per cubic foot?

MICROFILMING COSTS

1. *Camera rental:* 16mm rotary camera with 20:1 reduction ratio, rental at $50 per month
   (21 work days) .... $ 50.00

2. *Microfilm:* (16mm, 100′ rolls)

   $$\frac{20 \times 1{,}200}{11 + 1} = 2{,}000 \text{ images per roll}$$

   45,000 images ÷ 2,000 images per roll = 23 rolls

   23 rolls × $4.90 per roll cost including
   processing 112.70

3. *Preparation:* 15 days at $16 per day 240.00

4. *Actual filming time:* (750 exposures per hour less 15% fatigue factor × 7 hours per day = images filmed daily; images filmed daily ÷ into total images = days required)

   750 − 113 × 7 = 4,459 images filmed daily

   45,000 images ÷ 4,459 images =
   10 days' filming time

   *10 days' filming time at $16 per
   day 160.00

MISCELLANEOUS

*5. *Inspection, retakes, supervision, postage to processing center, etc.:* 6 days at $16 per day plus $1.00 postage .. 97.00

   Estimated cost of microfilming $659.70

*Note: Although this only adds up to 16 days, it will be necessary to keep the camera the full month because of the 3 or 4 days the film is being processed.

COST OF STORING IN ORIGINAL FORM

1. *Boxes:* (each box holds 12″ of records and costs 35¢)

   12″ × 100 documents per inch = 1,200 documents per box

   $$\frac{45{,}000 \text{ documents}}{1{,}200 \text{ documents per box}} = 38 \text{ boxes required}$$

   38 boxes × 35¢ per box = $12.30

   Cost of boxes .... $ 12.30

2. *Preparation time for packing boxes, preparing inventory, listings, etc.:* 3 days at $16 per day .... $ 48.00

3. *Cost of transportation* to commercial warehouse 18.00

4. *Warehouse labor-in charge:* 1 hour at $5 per hour 5.00

5. *Cost of storage of 38 boxes for 8 years* at $1.50 per year per box 459.00

   Cost of storage of records in commercial warehouse for maximum life of records $542.30

Conclusion. It would cost $117.40 less to store the Paid Accounts Receivable files in their original form in a commercial warehouse for their eight-year retention period than it would to microfilm them. Based upon the above costs, it would require an eleven-year retention period for these files before microfilming became economically feasible (before the costs of storage exceeded the costs of microfilming).

EXAMPLE OF WHEN *TO* MICROFILM

Problem. A large aerospace company currently retains its canceled Common Stock Certificates for twenty-one years. To save space, they are considering microfilming these certificates. Presently, there are 75,000 certificates, 8½" × 11", none of which are stapled. Rarely are these certificates ever referred to. (1) How much would it cost to microfilm these certificates? (2) How does this compare with storage of the original canceled certificates in the company's records center where space costs are $1.60 per cubic foot (including space, overhead, and maintenance)?

MICROFILMING COSTS

1. *Camera rental:* 16mm rotary camera with 24:1 reduction ratio, rental at $50 per month (5 weeks) .... $ 62.50

2. *Microfilm:* (16mm, 200′ rolls)

$$\frac{24 \times 2,400}{11 + 1} = 4,800 \text{ images per roll}$$

   75,000 images ÷ 4,800 images per roll = 16 rolls

   16 rolls at $7.50 per roll cost including processing 120.00

3. *Preparation:* 8 days at $16 per day $128.00

4. *Actual filming time:* (750 exposures per hour less 15% fatigue factor × 7 hours per day = images filmed daily; images filmed daily ÷ into total images = days required)

$$750 - 113 \times 7 = 4{,}459 \text{ images filmed daily}$$

$$75{,}000 \div 4{,}459 = 17 \text{ days filming time}$$

17 days filming time at $16 per day 272.00

5. *Inspection, retakes, supervision, etc.:* 3 days at $16 per day 48.00

6. *Postage to processing center* 2.00

Estimated cost of microfilming $632.50

Cost of Storing in Original Form

1. *Boxes:* (each box holds 12″ of records and costs 35¢) 12″ × 100 documents per inch = 1,200 documents per box

$$\frac{75{,}000 \text{ documents}}{1{,}200 \text{ documents per box}} = 63 \text{ boxes required}$$

63 boxes × 35¢ per box = $22.05

Cost of boxes ....$ 22.05

2. *Preparation time for packing boxes, preparing inventory, listings, etc.:* 2 days at $16 per day 32.00

3. *Cost of transporting boxes to records center* 18.00

4. *Cost of storing 63 boxes for 21 years* at $1.60 per year per box 2,116.80

Cost of storage of records in company records center for maximum life of records $2,188.85

Conclusion. Microfilming these files is economically justified since the costs of microfilming will be $1,556.35 less than the costs of retaining the records in their original form in a company records center for the records' retention period.

Chapter 6

Microfilm Procedures

In previous chapters, we have discussed reasons for using microfilm in controlling business records, and also some situations where the use of microfilm is *not likely* to prove economical. We have also mentioned various types of microfilm, or microforms, that are available, and tried to show how they can be adapted to information storage and retrieval situations, ranging from the simple to the very complex. But the records manager who has not previously used microfilm will probably be most interested in simple methods for getting a microfilm program under way. He is probably staring every day at rows of file cabinets containing tons of aging records that are seldom referred to.

Exactly what must be done in the office to get these documents on film? Then, what is a simple but effective indexing procedure that will enable clerical personnel to locate any document with reasonable ease whenever it should be needed? Remember, we are not talking about an active daily reference situation—just occasional reference. Quicker systems for frequent reference will be discussed later in this chapter.

Our initial purpose is to provide a plan of operation for getting a simple microfilm program involving 16mm roll microfilm under way. We will assume that filming will be done in company offices by the clerical staff and that the processing will be handled by an outside service company. This is logical because any one of a number of good rotary cameras are inexpensive to buy or rent, and they can be easily operated by office personnel. The more complicated details of processing are best handled by an outside service company except in special situations (not the type we are now discussing) where the need for speed or great volume of work makes an in-company processing facility economical. The only problems that should occur will be in the physical handling of the documents and putting a simple indexing system into use.

INDEXING

Because each microfilm roll will contain so many documents, it is especially important that an effective indexing system be decided upon. This system need not be elaborate, all-inclusive, expensive, or too detailed. All that is needed is a method of dividing a microfilm roll into readily identifiable parts, thus facilitating reference to any document contained on that roll. At Olin Mathieson Chemical Corporation, a large and diversified company with complicated information storage needs, it was found that the common target (or flash) card technique was applicable in nearly all cases involving roll microfilm indexing. This is the method that will be described and illustrated here. The sample targets illustrated at the end of this chapter, or similar cards, are available from manufacturers of microfilm equipment and other sources.

Documents such as invoices or checks that have a numerical sequence are particularly easy to locate after their approximate position has been determined by locating the nearest filing sequence target. With other types of documents, it may be advisable to number them before or during microfilming. Some rotary cameras are equipped with attachments that number documents before the image is recorded on film. The type and volume of the documents and probable frequency of reference are factors to be considered in determining whether it is necessary to number all documents in addition to identifying areas of reference by filing sequence targets that show alphabetical or numerical areas.

Overall, the target card system is simple enough to be quickly understood from the illustrations that follow. First, the flash cards are shown in diagrams in relation to the recorded documents on strips of roll microfilm. The drawings also suggest the frequency with which the various identifying target cards should be inserted in a roll of microfilmed records. Also included are models of commonly used flash cards that the records manager may use as models for designing his own. Other illustrations show sample Table of Contents forms that may be affixed to roll microfilm containers and work sheet forms for the microfilming operation.

MODEL INDEXING PLAN

Indexing for Normal Filmings

Figure 6–1 shows areas after each 25 feet of film that, along with title targets, permit identification of the records contained on the film, as well as rapid, accurate reference to any individual record.

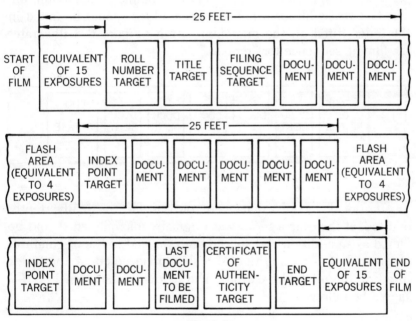

Fig. 6–1.

Indexing for Corrections

Occasionally, the camera operator may notice that a document has been incorrectly filmed. It may have been twisted, folded, or torn. In such cases, a Correction Target is photographed immediately after the incorrect document, and it is immediately refilmed. This target is illustrated in Fig. 6–2.

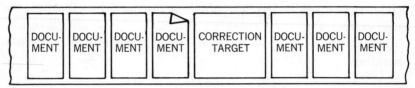

Fig. 6–2.

Indexing for Retakes and Additions

Upon inspection of a processed microfilm roll, you may notice that certain documents are illegible or incorrectly photographed (torn, bent, or twisted). Such documents should be rephotographed and spliced onto the end of the completed microfilm roll. The fact that additional film has been added should be noted in the index listed on the microfilm carton. Figure 6–3 illustrates the filming sequence for "retakes."

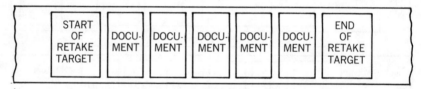

Fig. 6–3.

Additional records that were out of file, or inadvertently omitted, at the time a series was originally microfilmed should be filmed as an addition and spliced onto the end of the original roll of microfilm. This addition also should be noted in the index listed on the microfilm carton. The sequence shown in Fig. 6–4 should be followed.

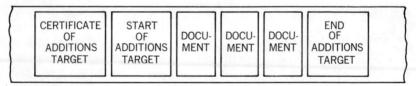

Fig. 6–4.

GETTING READY

Try to set up the microfilm camera as close as possible to the records to be microfilmed. This will serve several purposes:

1. Reduce time spent transporting records to and from the microfilm camera's location.
2. Make the records being microfilmed readily available for reference while they are out-of-files awaiting filming.
3. Help to insure that the records are returned to the proper place after filming.

Whether or not it is possible to set up the microfilm camera in the general area of the records, someone from the department requesting microfilm service should be assigned to assist the camera operator in his work. This person will be responsible for (1) identifying the records to be filmed; (2) removing them from the files; (3) removing all pins, staples, and paper clips prior to filming; (4) unfolding all records and arranging them in the same direction; (5) restapling, repinning, refolding, and reclipping records (as required) after filming; (6) refiling records to be retained in the office after filming; and (7) setting aside records to be transferred to an inactive storage area or destroyed after microfilming. Cooperation by individual departments through the assignment of staff members to assist the operator enables him to devote the bulk of his time to his main task—microfilming. In addition, it also reduces the possibility of wrong papers being refastened together, misfiling, etc.

A combination procedure checklist and work sheet similar to the Microfilm Index (see Fig. 6–5) is also very useful. This has a twofold purpose:

1. To assure that the necessary operating preliminaries (winding film, cleaning glass, making adjustments, etc.) are performed before any actual filming takes place.
2. To provide a source document for preparing the Table of Contents labels that will be used with each microfilm roll (see Fig. 6–6). This form will also prove valuable if your microfilm is not satisfactory and you find it necessary to refilm one or more documents. In such a case, all you need to do is compare the Microfilm Index with the microfilm roll, determine which records did not reproduce clearly, and refilm them.

MICROFILM INDEX

DEPARTMENT   REEL NUMBER

☐ CLEAN GLASS   ☐ WIND FILM 10 TURNS   ☐ ADJUST SETTING   ☐ SET COUNTER AT ZERO   ☐ CHECK FILM TAKE-UP

NO.	RECORD TITLE	COUNTER READING (FINAL)	NO.	RECORD TITLE	COUNTER READING (FINAL)
1	ROLL NUMBER TARGET		17		
2	TITLE TARGET		18		
3	FILING SEQUENCE TARGET		19		
4			20		
5			21		
6			22		
7			23		
8			24		
9			25		
10			26		
11			27		
12			28		
13			29		
14			30		
15			31		
16			32		

Fig. 6–5. Microfilm checklist and work sheet.

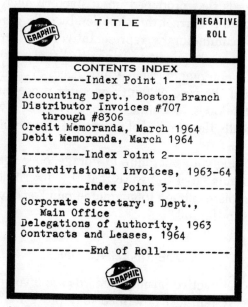

Fig. 6–6. Index label for box of roll microfilm that lists contents and provides reference markers.

AFTER MICROFILMING

Do not destroy any records until you have had a chance to review the processed microfilm rolls containing copies of those records. For simplicity, the records should be stored in the order in which they were microfilmed in cardboard transfiles that are marked with the number of the microfilm roll. Then, after the film has been returned from the processing laboratory, inspected, and found satisfactory, these original records can be disposed of in accordance with local procedure (either destroyed, sent to a storage area, or returned to files).

Be sure, however, to carefully inspect each roll of microfilm upon its return. If you have any doubts concerning the ability of any particular image to reproduce a usable copy, make one on the spot. If it is unsatisfactory, immediately refilm the document and, upon its return from the processing laboratory, splice it onto the end of the roll containing the defective image. If you find that you frequently are faced with the problem and expense of refilming records that produced unsatisfactory microimages, you should immediately correct this situation by calling in your microfilm camera manufacturer's representative. This representative will examine your equipment and operating procedure and (in the case of faulty equipment) make any necessary adjustments or recommend (in the case of faulty operator procedures) changes in filming techniques. In either case, this service will normally reduce drastically the number of unacceptable microimages in the future.

Before sending your microfilm to storage, once again check the Table of Contents label to assure that the description contained thereon is complete enough to guarantee rapid, accurate reference to documents in the roll.

CODE LINE INDEXING

In cases where active business records are involved, the target card indexing system just described may prove too slow for efficient and economical reference to microfilmed records. In such cases, a system such as a Recordak Kodamatic indexing system may be the answer to the problem. This system has been in use for many years in widely diversified retailing, wholesaling, and manufacturing records-keeping operations. It played an important role in spreading the use of high-speed microfilming techniques outside their original application in the banking field. Under this system, documents are microfilmed by a rotary camera that is equipped with tiny adjustable internal spotlights that are focused on the sides of the film as images are registered on it. These flashing lights register a code made up of variously positioned bar images that identify the document by numerical sequence.

When the film is later viewed in a microfilm reader, these high-density stripes appear as solid dark index lines. To permit the coding (or sectionalizing) into easily identifiable segments to be quickly read, a code scale corresponding to the pattern used in registering the stripes on the film will be found at the side of the screen on Recordak Lodestar readers and reader-printers (Fig. 6-7). This refinement enables the viewer to scan a roll of microfilm at high speed for a particular section of the film, or a particular document. He does not try to read documents, even as he gets near the end of this search. The position of the stripes or bars on the side of the film allows him to quickly distinguish documents. To find what he is looking for, he may have to actually scan only a few frames of film.

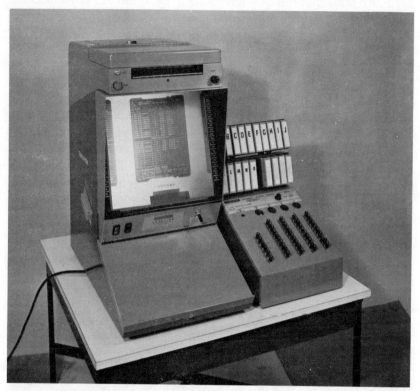

Fig. 6–7. Recordak Lodestar reader-printer shown with image control keyboard. Magazines holding 16mm microfilm are stacked above keyboard.

IMAGE CONTROL INDEXING

More complete automation of microfilm search procedures can be obtained by a system known as image control indexing. It works as follows. At the time of microfilming, an index code number is assigned to each document. This index number, which can run into the tens of thousands, appears alongside the microfilmed document as a group of "blips" arranged in a gridiron pattern. When reference to any document contained on a roll of image control indexed microfilm is required, the microfilm is inserted into a microfilm reader to which a special accessory unit, an image control keyboard, has been linked. The searcher merely enters the index code number of the desired document on the keyboard, and that roll of microfilm will be automatically searched at high speed, and the appropriate image will be registered on the viewing screen. A copy of such an image can be obtained by pushing the PRINT button on an attached reader-printer.

OTHER INDEXING SYSTEMS

Methods and techniques of indexing microfilm mounted in aperture cards and of coding tabulating cards to facilitate the location of microfilmed documents dealing with specific subjects are described in Chapters 3 and 7, respectively. These are two important indexing systems. Another system is the photomemory system using binary code indexing. This is discussed in greater detail in Chapter 7.

Fig. 6–8. A microfilm indexing system known as "Microstrip" designed for ready access to files of limited volume. Strips of 16mm microfilm are mounted in cardboard "frames" that allow them to be easily handled and inserted in the specially designed reader. This is a Recordak product.

SUPPLEMENTAL LOCATOR INDEXING

It should be pointed out that any microfilm system using roll or chip film will require an additional index—one that will initially direct you to the units of film containing the documents you desire. Depending upon the complexity of indexing and classifying you wish to do, as well as the number of rolls or chip magazines of microfilm involved, this supplemental locator index can range from a small box of 3″ × 5″ index cards to a complex system involving key punched tabulating cards.

The important point to remember concerning a locator system is that it can be designed to fit the problem. There is no need to be locked into a machine-driven system unless the difficulty of thoroughly searching a file warrants it.

SCHEDULING MICROFILMING PROJECTS

It is recommended that you develop a schedule that lists the tentative dates in each month when recurring microfilming projects will be performed. This will permit effective use of microfilming personnel and equipment and reduce overtime and the number of "crash" jobs by leveling out the peaks and valleys of demand for microfilming services.

In addition, scheduling recurring microfilming projects in advance will highlight those situations in which additional microfilming cannot be fitted into the workload. Alternatives such as the following can then be selected.

1. The work must be performed on overtime.
2. The work must be performed by temporarily hired or assigned personnel, using available or specially leased equipment.
3. The work must be performed by an outside service company.

Knowledge of these facts when estimating the costs of nonrecurring microfilming projects will enable the records manager to develop realistic, reliable cost estimates.

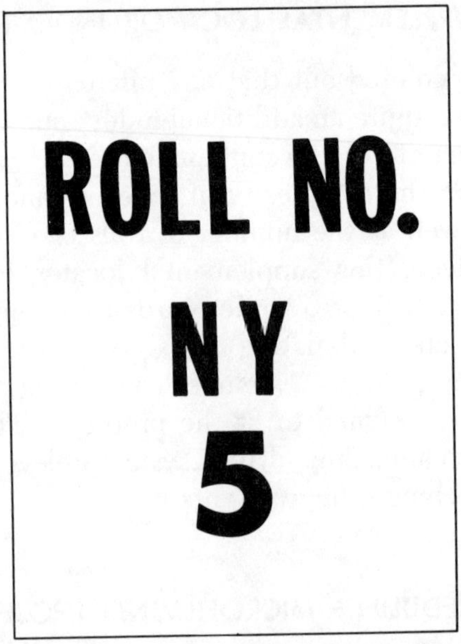
ROLL NO.
NY
5

Fig. 6–9. Roll number target. Provides each microfilm roll with a numerical identification large enough to be read without magnification to insure that it is returned to its proper carton after viewing. Filmed as the first document on each roll.

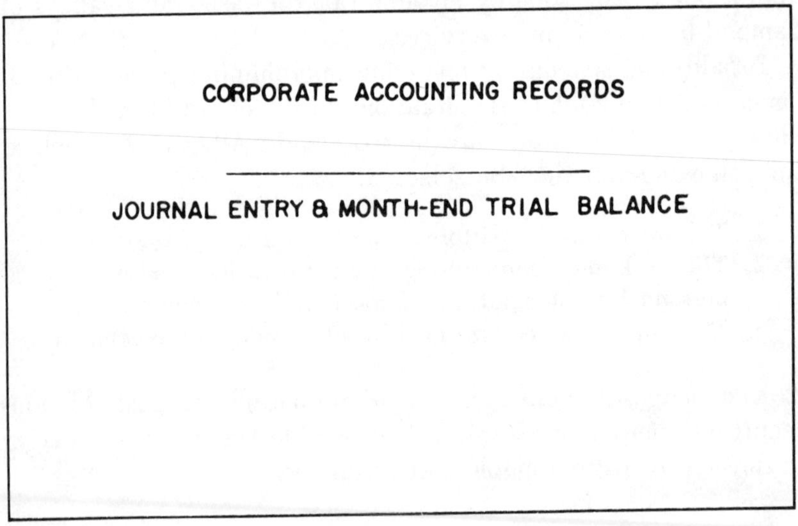
CORPORATE ACCOUNTING RECORDS

JOURNAL ENTRY & MONTH-END TRIAL BALANCE

Fig. 6–10. Title target. Identifies the records contained on the microfilm roll. Filmed as the second document on each roll.

FILING SEQUENCE NUMERICAL

Fig. 6–11. Filing sequence target. Explains file arrangement and sequence. Filmed on each roll following the title target.

INDEX POINT

2

Fig. 6–12. Index point target. Used to facilitate reference. Index Point "1" is positioned immediately after the first flash area at the end of 25 feet of film; Index Point "2" is positioned immediately after the second flash area at the end of 50 feet of film; etc.

CORRECTION

THIS DOCUMENT

HAS BEEN REPHOTOGRAPHED

TO ASSURE LEGIBILITY

Fig. 6–13. Correction target. Indicates an improperly filmed document has been refilmed. Microfilmed immediately after a document has been incorrectly photographed (torn, twisted, or bent documents). The correction target is followed by a retake of the original document.

CERTIFICATE OF AUTHENTICITY

THIS IS TO CERTIFY that the microfilms appearing on this Film-File

Starting with_____and

Ending with_____are

accurate and complete reproductions of records of _____ ,

_____ Division, delivered to the undersigned by _____ ,

_____ of _____ ,

the legal custodian of said records, who affirmed that such records were received or made by said

Division. Said records were microfilmed by the undersigned in the regular course of business

pursuant to established company policy of said Corporation to maintain and preserve such records

through the storage of microfilm reproductions thereof in protected locations.

It is further certified that the photographic processes used for micro-

filming of the above records were accomplished in a manner and on microfilm which meets with the

requirements of the National Bureau of Standards for permanent microphotographic copy.

DATE PRODUCED *(Month, day, year)*	BY *(Camera Operator)*
PLACE *(City and state)*	

Fig. 6–14. Certificate of authenticity and declaration of intent. States company's practice of microfilming business records and authenticates all documents on the microfilm roll as true copies for legal or audit purposes. Microfilmed after the last document in series to be filmed.

END

Fig. 6–15. End target. Indicates end of particular series of records. Photographed as last document on roll, immediately after certificate of authenticity.

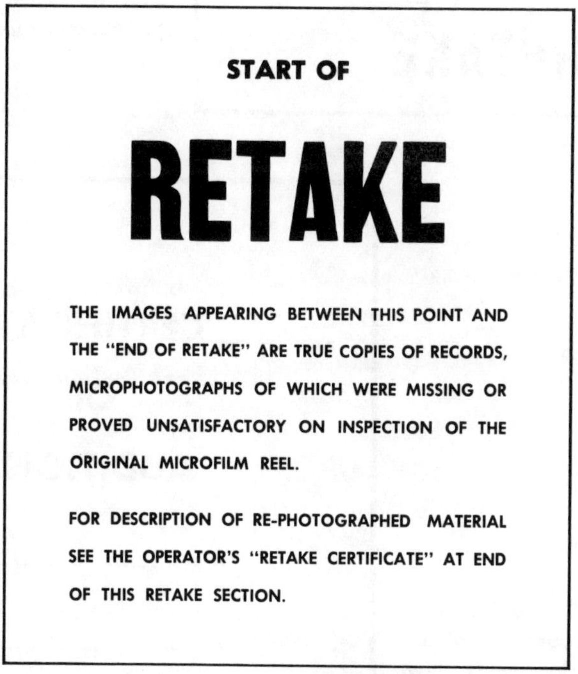

START OF

RETAKE

THE IMAGES APPEARING BETWEEN THIS POINT AND THE "END OF RETAKE" ARE TRUE COPIES OF RECORDS, MICROPHOTOGRAPHS OF WHICH WERE MISSING OR PROVED UNSATISFACTORY ON INSPECTION OF THE ORIGINAL MICROFILM REEL.

FOR DESCRIPTION OF RE-PHOTOGRAPHED MATERIAL SEE THE OPERATOR'S "RETAKE CERTIFICATE" AT END OF THIS RETAKE SECTION.

Fig. 6–16. Start of retake target. Explains the reasons for refilming documents that will subsequently be spliced at the end of a complete roll of microfilm. This target is filmed immediately before the documents to be rephotographed.

JOB NO.

REEL NO.

RETAKE CERTIFICATE

I HEREBY CERTIFY THAT THE MICRO-PHOTOGRAPHS APPEARING BETWEEN
"START OF RETAKE" AND THIS "RETAKE CERTIFICATE" ARE TRUE COPIES OF THE
ORIGINAL DOCUMENTS DESCRIBED BELOW.

DATE

SIGNATURE OF CAMERA OPERATOR

END OF
RETAKE

Fig. 6–17. End of retake target. Indicates end of the retake section and avoids confusion with rest of microfilm images. Also certifies as to authenticity of refilmed documents. Filmed immediately after last document to be rephotographed.

CERTIFICATE
OF
ADDITIONS

Reason_____

Item_____

Fig. 6–18. Certificate of additions target. Indicates additional documents have been added to the microfilm roll. Identifies the documents and describes reason for their separate filming.

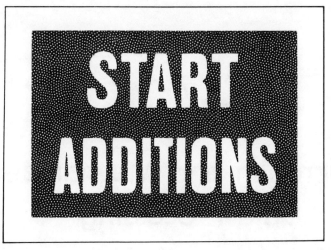

Fig. 6–19. Start additions target. Filmed immediately after the certificate of additions. Alerts the viewer to the documents following.

Fig. 6–20. End additions target. Filmed after the last additional document to be filmed.

Chapter 7

Microfilm and Mechanized Data Processing

Originally, business applications of microfilm were limited to saving space through the reduction of bulky files of inactive documents. It is only since World War II that microfilm has really emerged from the records storage area and taken its place as an active business systems tool. Today, surprising systems improvements are being accomplished that involve the use of data processing equipment in conjunction with microfilm.

Early systems for the retrieval of information stored on microfilm were usually simple but tended to be time-consuming. Generally, some indexing method was set up to indicate to the requestor which rolls of microfilm contained the records he wanted to examine. The normal indexing method was to prepare a detailed listing of the contents of each microfilm roll on either index cards or in a notebook. Whenever reference was required, it was necessary to search these indexes to determine which rolls of films should be checked. As with any manual system, this method tended to be inefficient and expensive. Human errors were frequent; all pertinent data might or might not be retrieved from the microfilm rolls. Companies hesitated to use microfilm for other than inactive records to which reference was limited.

As time passed, a number of semiautomatic indexing and coding systems were developed to locate information on roll microfilm, notably the systems developed by Recordak for use with that company's equipment. These retrieval systems led to much wider use of microfilm, since they were designed for use with current business records. They range from methods whereby a simple bar code is recorded on the microfilm image and lined up on the reader screen to quite complicated retrieval apparatus such as the "Miracode" equipment that has only recently come into use (Fig. 7–1). This system allows the operator to automatically

Fig. 7–1. This array of equipment includes (*left*) a file of 16mm roll micro-film magazines, (*center*) a Recordak reader-printer, and (*right*) an electronic keyboard device that is programmed to locate documents in 16mm roll micro-film magazines when descriptive numbers are keyed into it.

search the file for broad categories and subcategories of documents that have been cross-indexed. Miracode might be said to bridge the gap between simple roll microfilm indexing and the computer-controlled information retrieval systems used by large corporations and government agencies. Operation of the system depends on binary code "blips" printed on the film to identify groups of document images.

But microfilm information retrieval systems are by no means limited to these. If a company has available unit record key punch tabulating equipment, it can use this hardware in a system that will answer very complicated questions about the contents of the large microfilm files. Computers, if the job warrants it, can also be employed. Once a cross-indexing plan is correctly translated into a punched card index, the machines can take over the task of locating information.

The key to a workable microfilm system using tabulating cards and machines is to be able to reduce the information contained in a particular document to machine-storable terms to permit searching and selection by mechanical means. Before this is done, it is necessary to develop a "thesaurus" (or listing) of subjects and modifying descriptions into which each document will be classified. This is usually accomplished by having a technical librarian scan a group of documents and note the various subjects discussed in the documents along with any pertinent modifiers.

For example, a document may be concerned with the frequency of accidents sustained by female electronics assemblers in a company's Ohio plant during the quarter-year ending June 30, 1965. The subject discussed here is *accidents*. The specific facet of the subject is the *frequency of accidents*. However, the document is concerned only with *frequency of accidents* for *female electronics workers* at the *Ohio plant* during the *quarter-year ending June 30, 1965*. Such a document might be coded as follows:

Subject:	accidents
Primary modifier:	frequency of accidents
Secondary modifiers:	female electronics assemblers
	Ohio plant
	quarter-year ending June 30, 1965

Each document would be scanned and indexed in this manner. When enough documents have been indexed to provide a representative sampling of the type of subjects generally described in the documents to be microfilmed (here judgment is usually the determining factor as to when that point has been reached), each subject is listed in alphabetical order. A consecutive numerical code number is arbitrarily assigned to each subject, for example:

0001	Accidents
0002	Applications
0003	Bargaining Units
0004	Contracts
0005	Diseases
0006	Equipment

Then each primary modifier would be arranged in alphabetic order, and a consecutive numeric code assigned to each. Likewise, each secondary modifier would be arranged in alphabetic order, and a consecutive numeric code assigned.

As each subsequent document is scanned, the indexing and coding librarian will note across the top of the first page the index numbers of the various subjects and modifiers discussed in the document.

These documents are then forwarded for microfilming. After microfilming, the camera operator groups together all documents contained on the same microfilm roll. He then places a rubber band around each group and sends them on to the key-punch department. Here one or more tabulating cards are prepared for each document, depending upon the number of subjects and primary and secondary modifiers involved. A typical card layout might be as follows:

Card Column	Data
1–5	Subject
10–15	Primary Modifier
15–20	Secondary Modifier

Naturally, if more than one subject, primary modifier, and secondary modifier is coded on a document, there will be more than one tabulating card prepared for that document.

Finally, the microfilm roll number is key-punched into the tabulating card. The documents are then held, pending examination of the processed microfilm, and the tabulating cards are filed for machine reference (unless retrieval is to be by computer, in which case the tab cards may be used as the source of a magnetic tape record).

When reference is made, the tabulating cards (or computer tapes if that is the method of storage) are matched against keyed-in codes representing the desired information. Any matching codes ("hits") represent documents that should be searched further to determine if the specific information desired is contained therein. The microfilm roll numbers of such documents are also noted. This information is then relayed to the microfilm library, and a search of the pertinent rolls of microfilm is made. If copies of microimages are desired, these are obtained from a reader-printer.

PHOTOMEMORY SYSTEMS

Recently, several information retrieval systems that unitize documents and their corresponding indexing on the same chip or section of microfilm have been developed. While these systems do not provide a completely self-contained information retrieval system, they have reduced much of the time involved in locating a document under the system described above by providing for multiple coding of the same document, thereby allowing for greater indexing in depth and retrieval based upon more selective processes.

However, as with all microfilm systems, these photomemory systems still require an index to refer you to the rolls or containers containing the desired documents. Still this is much quicker than if the documents had to be located manually using a reader-printer.

Other photomemory systems currently available are set up in the same general manner. The process begins when the camera operator lays the document to be microfilmed upon the filming surface of a planetary microfilm camera. Then, referring to the numeric coding on the document, the operator keys in the pertinent indexing on a special coding machine. This coding machine then creates a code that is entered into the microfilm either in front of the documents to be filmed (as in the case of Miracode) or on the same length of film occupied by the documents to be filmed (as in the case of MEDIA). With Miracode, the indexing is across the width of the microfilm; with MEDIA, it is across the length.

When reference is required, it is first necessary to determine which microfilm magazines or rolls should be searched. Then the selected magazines or rolls are placed in a searching reference unit, and the code numbers of the desired data are keyed in. The microimages are then mechanically scanned at a rate of approximately 16 feet per second. Whenever the code keyed into the selector is encountered on the microfilm, the selector either stops its scanning and flashes the enlarged document on a viewing screen (in the case of Miracode) or segregates the film chip containing the desired coding from those that do not (in the case of MEDIA). If, after viewing, copies of these documents are desired, they may be obtained by using printers that are integrated with the equipment.

USING COMPUTERS

Large-capacity microfilm retrieval systems can also be devised that employ computers already available in a company. A Midwestern chemical firm used this approach for the storage and retrieval of its Management Inventory of Skills file. This repository of information, which consists of job performance and appraisal reports, personnel questionnaire forms, and skills inventory questionnaires, is the basic tool for its management development program.

Active files such as these must be continually updated and, because of the variety of documents and information contained in them, are difficult and expensive to maintain. Also, the data involved must be reviewed by a number of individuals in different locations before decisions can be reached. To design an efficient information retrieval system to handle this situation, the company turned to a manual microfilm aperture cards file cross-indexed on computer tape.

Each of the hard-copy records in individual employee files was examined and coded to reflect significant data concerning the employee. The following were included:

Payroll identification number
Marital status
Citizenship
Degrees held
Foreign languages spoken
Work experience
Years of supervisory or management experience
Work specialty
Geographic preferences
Performance evaluations

Numerical codes were assigned to each of the items of information listed for each employee. For instance, under marital status, the numeral 2 would indicate single; 3 would mean married; and 4, divorced or separated. Under degrees, 1 would indicate a B.A.; 3, a Master's; etc.

The individual documents in each employee's file were then microfilmed, and the 35mm film records were mounted in standard aperture cards. Because of the large quantity of information that needed to be coded on each employee, it was not feasible to enter the coding data on the aperture cards. In addition, placing the information units on magnetic tape numerically keyed to the aperture cards made searching of the files a considerably faster process.

The searching procedure is approximately as follows: An indexer determines the code numbers of the particular aptitudes sought. For instance, the need might be for a mechanical engineer with at least three years' experience, supervisory job experience, and willingness to relocate in Montana. These codes are fed into the computer for comparison with the entries on the tape file. The computer then prints out the names of employees meeting the requirements.

This printout is sent to the Management Development Department where the aperture cards corresponding to the names are pulled from the microfilm files. Duplicate cards are made on diazo equipment, and the master cards are returned to the file. These duplicate cards can then be forwarded to the persons responsible for reviewing files of potential applicants for the position in question. These reviewers examine the microfilmed documents with desk-top readers.

In addition to the speed and ease of reference this system affords, it has two further advantages: low cost of preparing and mailing duplicate employee files from one office to another, and assurance that the master files will remain intact, since only duplicate aperture cards leave the office.

OPTICAL SCANNING

Still another application is one in which microfilm and data processing equipment are effectively combined in the use of optical scanning equipment (machines that read). Perhaps the best single example of such a system is the FOSDIC (Film Optical

Sensing Device for Input to Computers) system developed by the U.S. Weather Bureau.

This agency had a library of over 300,000 tabulating cards containing data used to answer meteorological questions. The repository of tab cards was growing at a rate of over 10 per cent annually. In addition, the cards would wear out within several years and, conceivably, could be lost or destroyed. Also, the input speed of the tabulating cards into the Weather Bureau's computers was far less than the operating capacity of the computers.

The Weather Bureau therefore turned to microfilm to solve these three basic defects of the tabulating card system. And solve them they did in the following manner:

1. *Space.* Each microfilm roll was capable of holding the images of 13,000 tabulating cards, resulting in a 150:1 reduction in space requirements.
2. *Loss or damage.* Microfilm, with proper care, is relatively permanent and less subject to loss than are tabulating cards.
3. *Input speed.* Microfilm can be fed into computers at far greater speeds than can tabulating cards, thus making greater use of the computers' operating speeds.

The method whereby microfilmed tab cards can out-speed magnetic tape in the FOSDIC system is not complicated. Tabulating cards are photographed by a high-speed camera. In this photography, the image is distorted somewhat by an anomorphic lens (the same type as used in projecting CinemaScope motion pictures). The result is that the microfilm image of the cards is "stretched" so that it appears longer than normal and the punch holes appear to be almost square. This permits fitting of more cards to an inch of film, and enables the round electronic beam of an optical scanning device to sense the holes more easily.

For purposes of data processing, a role of microfilm then assumes the same functions as a roll of magnetic tape. But the camera is able to pack 850 alphanumeric characters into each linear inch of 16mm film. This represents a data density at least five times that of magnetic tape systems in use at the time the FOSDIC microfilm retrieval system was developed.

Other systems wherein microfilm has advantages over magnetic tape in computer operations are in use. Notable examples are data processing systems that must reproduce and store graphic information such as diagrams, charts, and visual simulations of complicated production and traffic control activities. In these cases, it is more efficient to maintain a compact "real" image on microfilm than to resort to a clumsy process of reducing this image to machine language for storage.

Chapter 8

Cameras

There are two types of cameras commonly used in microfilming operations. One is the rotary camera, usually a boxlike piece of equipment into which documents can be fed at high speed. The documents are recorded on film as they pass in front of a slitlike aperture. The other is the planetary camera in which the film unit is suspended over a flat copyboard.

ROTARY CAMERAS

The rotary camera is much more compact than the planetary camera and is capable of far greater output—many thousands of images per hour, depending on the efficiency of the machine and the clerk feeding documents into it. Rotary cameras generally cost less than planetary cameras, and smaller models are roughly the size of a portable typewriter. Generally, the exposure is preset; all that is necessary is to feed documents into the camera. Actual speed of operation varies from about 600 documents per hour (clerk hand-feeding letter-size sheets) to about 4,000 per hour (checks mechanically fed into machine).

Documents are fed (either manually or by an automatic feeding attachment) through an opening in the front of the camera. As the documents pass through the opening, they are usually pressed against a continuously moving belt that carries them into position for filming. In the film unit of the rotary camera, film also moves synchronously with the paper documents. This makes it possible to film a document while it is moving, greatly increasing the speed of the operation. An internal lighting system, adjustable for reflectance characteristics of various colors of paper documents, provides the light for filming. Since the focus of the lens is fixed, the brightness adjustment is one of the few necessary manipulations.

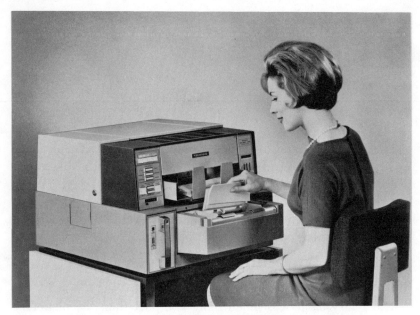

Fig. 8–1. Recordak "Reliant 600" rotary camera.

Machines such as the one shown in Fig. 8–1 are the workhorses of office microfilming operations. Their intake belts feed a continuous stream of letters, invoices, and similar records into the unit where they are automatically photographed on 16mm roll film. A wide variety of attachments are available that will number, code, and imprint documents just before they are photographed. Operation is simple and clerical personnel can be quickly trained to handle a rotary camera.

A fairly important advantage of the rotary camera is that it can accept a document of any length for filming, provided the width of the document is not wider than the camera's intake feed, which is usually 12 inches. Since the shutter of a rotary camera is trig-

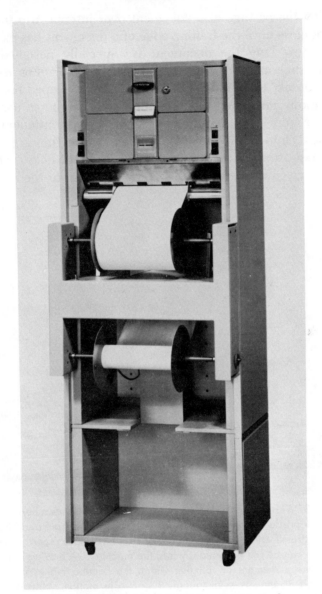

Fig. 8–2. The Bell & Howell Tab-Tronic is an automatic flow camera designed to make a 16mm film record of the continuous forms that are the printout of data processing equipment. Its primary advantage is that all the information on the bulky continuous forms can be stored on a compact roll of film.

gered by the passage of a document over internal trip fingers, it will not close until the trailing edge of a document has passed, no matter how long the document is. Specially designed rotary cameras such as the Bell & Howell "Tab-Tronic" (Fig. 8–2) and the Recordak "Rotomatic" (Fig. 8–3) were developed for systems applications involving the microfilming of unburst continuous forms. Figure 8–4a depicts how a clerk can continuously feed documents into a desk-top flow camera and how they are returned just as fast after passing between short conveyor belts. The electrically driven conveyor belts are synchronized to the movement

Fig. 8–3. This is a portable flow camera. The model shown here (Recordak) and similar products from other manufacturers offer a simple and inexpensive method of transferring almost any kind of standard office record to microfilm. Documents can be fed continuously into the machine. A moving belt synchronized to the movement of roll film within the camera makes it possible to photograph documents even though they are in motion. Necessary adjustments are few, and the machine can be carried easily from room to room.

of the 16mm roll microfilm in the film unit. Both documents and film move through the optical train at constant speeds in relation to each other, making it possible to record in the same manner what would occur if both were standing still. Other rotary cameras can photograph both front and back of documents at

the same time (Fig. 8–4b). This is a great advantage in operations such as banking where records of countless thousands of
checks must be made economically and at high speed. The
duplex rotary camera films both sides of documents simultane-
ously by means of a mirror system that places two images side by
side on a single frame of 16mm film.

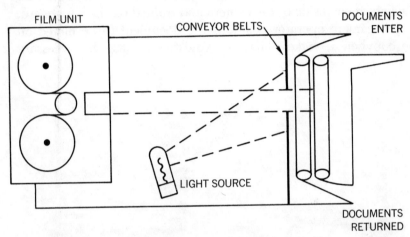

Fig. 8–4a. Simplified diagram of a small desk-top flow camera.

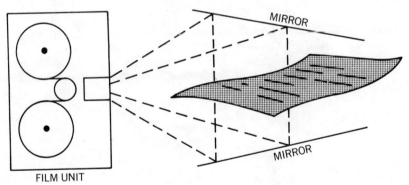

Fig. 8–4b. Simplified diagram of the duplex rotary camera.

The rotary camera is easy for office personnel to use, but it
has disadvantages. It will not accept bound documents or documents over a given width (usually 12 inches). Since its focal
length is fixed, the reduction ratio usually cannot be decreased to
obtain greater clarity in filming. However, some units have interchangeable lenses and film units of different focal lengths.

PLANETARY CAMERAS

The planetary camera is used for precision work, such as the filming of engineering drawings. The film unit is mounted on an upright shaft and can be moved up and down on this shaft so that the lens can take in a larger or smaller image area, depending on requirements. Two or more floodlights are usually mounted on brackets at each side of the camera and trained on the copyboard.

The camera operator positions the document to be filmed on the copyboard, makes whatever adjustments may be necessary

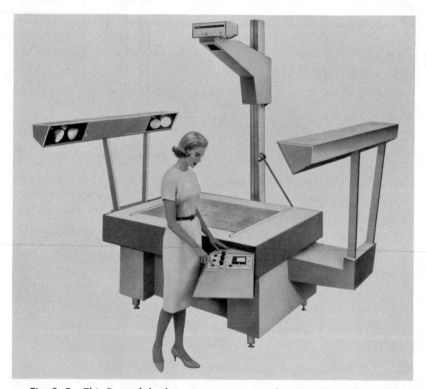

Fig. 8–5. This Recordak planetary camera is a large-size unit designed for the precision microfilming of documents such as engineering drawings. On this particular camera, six reduction ratios are standard, each obtained by push-button operation of a drive motor that raises or lowers the film unit. Focus is automatically adjusted as the film unit moves up or down. Exposure is controlled by a photocell that swings forward over the document on the camera bed and automatically retracts before exposure.

because of varying size or condition of the document, and activates the camera, usually by means of a foot switch that leaves his hands free. Since few adjustments are necessary in a routine filming operation, an operator can attain considerable speed, turning out 500 or more exposures per hour. When necessary, he can increase or decrease the reduction ratio, moving the camera higher or lower on its shaft, or he can introduce filters between camera lens and document in order to obtain better contrast in the film image. Also, most cameras are equipped with built-in exposure meters. (See Figs. 8–5 and 8–6.)

Most planetary cameras are designed for the use of 35mm film, either perforated or unperforated, but smaller and larger film sizes, (16mm, 70mm and 105mm film widths) are used in some applications. An example of a large-film planetary camera is the

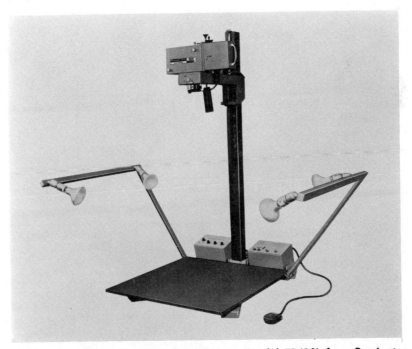

Fig. 8–6. This smaller planetary camera (Model F1410) from Remington Office Systems Division of Sperry Rand Corporation is designed to meet the needs of business and government facilities where deeds and large-size legal documents are recorded on 35mm film. It has a photocell device for exposure control and is capable of filming at variable reduction ratios from 12 through 20.

Price Range	Manufacturer	Model	Film Sizes	Filming Capability
A. Under $1,500.00	Documat, Inc.	Canon 1A	16mm	Simplex
		Canon 1A	16mm	Duplex Duo
	Federal Division of Victoreen Instrument Co.	MF-16	16mm	Simplex
	Itek Business Products	Portable	16mm	Simplex
	3M Co.	Sixteen	16mm	Simplex
	Recordak Corp.	RP-1	16mm	Simplex
B. Over $1,500.00	Bell & Howell Co.	Director 1	16mm	Simplex
		Tab-Tronic 575	16mm	Simplex
	Itek Business Products	42	16mm 35mm	Simplex
	Recordak Corp.	Reliant 500	16mm	Simplex Duplex Duo

Fig. 8–7. Classified directory

Reduction Ratio	Special Features and Attachments	Manufacturer's Rated Operating Speed
16:1 ⎯⎯ 34.5:1	Can film documents from 2″ × 3″ up to 8½″ × any continuous length. Camera is equipped with a footage indicator. Requires 110 volts, 60-cycle power source.	Up to 3,000 exposures per hour, depending upon size of documents filmed and method of feeding documents into camera.
24:1	Can film documents up to 11⅞″ × any continuous length. Camera is equipped with footage indicator.	85 linear feet per minute.
22.5:1	Can film documents up to 11″ × any continuous length. Camera is equipped with an exposure counter.	150 linear feet of paper per minute.
24:1	Can film documents up to 11⅞″ × any continuous length. Odemeter indexing system standard with this camera, as is footage indicator.	85 linear feet per minute.
20:1	A lightweight portable camera. Can film documents up to 12″ × any continuous length. Camera is equipped with an exposure counter, film footage indicator, and film warning signal. Two rolls of film can be exposed simultaneously. Film units are removable and interchangeable.	Up to 7,500 exposures per hour, depending upon size of documents filmed and method of feeding documents into camera.
24:1 34:1 44:1	Built-in automatic feeder and built-in 3-digit indexing meter and 6-digit item counter are standard equipment. Interchangeable lenses, endorser-printer, and automatic exposure control are optional.	Up to 7,200 images per hour, depending upon size of documents filmed and method of feeding documents into camera.
24:1	Basically used for microfilming computer printout. Films documents up to 15″ × any continuous length.	150 linear feet per minute.
20:1 35:1	Can film documents up to 42″ × any continuous length. Camera is equipped with exposure counter and end-of-film warning signal.	150 linear feet per minute.
24:1 32:1 40:1	Can film documents up to 12″ × any continuous length. Camera is equipped with a footage indicator and end-of-film warning signal. Integral indexing system (Kodamatic Indexing) standard with this camera. Two rolls of film can be exposed simultaneously. Film units are removable and interchangeable.	Up to 30,000 exposures per hour, depending upon size of documents filmed and method of feeding documents into camera.

of rotary cameras.

Price Range	Manufacturer	Model	Film Sizes	Filming Capability
B. Over $1,500.00 (*cont'd*)	Remington Office Systems Division of Sperry Rand Corp.	Film-A-Record 555	16mm	Simplex Duplex

Fig. 8–7.

Price Range	Manufacturer	Model	Film Sizes	Maximum Filming Capability
A. Under $1,500.00	Griscombe Products Corp.	A-1	35mm	20″ × 24″
	Remington Office Systems Division of Sperry Rand Corp.	F-35CR	35mm	20″ × 24″
		F-1100	16mm 35mm	24″ × 24″
B. $1,500.00 to $2,999.99	Atlantic Microfilm Corp.	X-Ray	35mm	14″ × 17″
	Griscombe Products Corp.	A-3	35mm	20″ × 24″
	Recordak Corp.	MRD-2	16mm 35mm	26″ × 36¾″
C. $3,000.00 to $5,999.99	Keuffel & Esser Co. (K & E)	52-2020	35mm	37½″ × 52½″

* See footnote on pp. 88–89.

Fig. 8–8. Classified directory

Reduction Ratio	Special Features and Attachments	Manufacturer's Rated Operating Speed
25:1 35:1 42:1	Can film documents up to 11″ × any continuous length. Camera is equipped with a footage indicator and end-of-film warning signal. Interchangeable lenses available.	125 linear feet per minute.

Concluded.

Reduction Ratio	Special Features and Attachments	Manufacturer's Rated Operating Speed
16:1	Exposure counter and light meter are available for use with this camera. End-of-film warning signal, light failure signal, and an improper threading alarm signal are standard on this camera.	❋
16:1	Exposure counter and light meter are available for use with this camera. End-of-film warning signal, light failure signal, and an improper threading alarm signal are standard on this camera.	❋
16:1 20:1	Footage indicator and end-of-film warning signal are standard with this camera.	❋
11:1	This camera is designed solely for the microfilming of X rays. It is equipped with a footage indicator as well as improper threading and end-of-film warning signals.	❋
16:1	End-of-film warning signal and footage indicator are standard with this camera.	❋
5:1 to 21:1	End-of-film warning signal, light meter, and footage indicator are standard with this camera. Available with 16mm conversion kit.	❋
12:1 to 30:1	Footage indicator, exposure counter, frame counter, and end-of-film warning signal are standard with this camera.	❋

of planetary cameras.

Price Range	Manufacturer	Model	Film Sizes	Maximum Filming Capability
C. $3,000.00 to $5,999.99 (cont'd)	3M Co.	1000d Camera/processor	35mm	18" × 24"
		Filmsort	35mm	24" × 36"
	Recordak Corp	C-3	16mm 35mm	37½" × 52½"
		D	16mm 35mm	26¼" × 36¼"
		E	16mm	22½" × 31½"
D. Over $6,000.00	Keuffel & Esser Co. (K & E)	52-2001	35mm 105mm	42" × 64"
	Recordak Corp.	MRG	35mm	45" × 63"

* Because of the many factors that can influence the rate of speed for planetary cameras (folded or rolled pages to be smoothed, operator proficiency, exposure adjustments required, etc.), it is not practical to carry rated speeds for this equip-

Fig. 8–8.

Reduction Ratio	Special Features and Attachments	Manufacturer's Rated Operating Speed
16:1	Capable of filming documents in premounted aperture cards and processing within 54-second cycle.	✳
16:1	Capable of filming up to eight 8½″ × 11″ documents in premounted aperture cards and processing within 45-second cycle.	✳
12:1 to 30:1	Available with 16mm conversion kit. Automatic focus change, light failure signal, end-of-film warning signal, and improper threading alarm signal are standard with this camera. Footage indicator and exposure counter are also standard.	✳
8:1 to 21:1	Using a special accessory copyboard, it is possible to film documents up to 37½″ × 52½″ at a 30:1 reduction ratio. Available with special accessory copyboard and 16mm conversion kit. Light meter and automatic focus change device are standard, as are footage indicator, exposure counter, light failure signal, end-of-film warning signal, and improper threading alarm signal.	✳
10:1 to 18:1	Lightweight, compact unit. Available with 16mm conversion kit and step-down transformer. Light meter and automatic focus change device are standard, as are footage indicator, exposure counter, light failure signal, end-of-film warning signal, and improper threading alarm signal.	✳
12:1 to 30:1	Exposure counter and end-of-film warning signal are standard with this camera.	✳
12:1 to 36:1	Footage indicator and end-of-film warning signal are standard with this camera.	✳

ment. All planetary cameras will perform at approximately the same speed (i.e., somewhere between 500 and 750 exposures per hour), but their greatest differences lie in their special features, attachments, and filming capabilities.

Concluded.

105mm model marketed by Keuffel & Esser for the making of sharp, low-reduction microfilm of large-size engineering drawings. But under most circumstances, wide film is not necessary, and practically all engineering drawing microfilm applications involve 35mm film. It is this size image that we commonly see mounted on aperture cards. There are many 35mm planetary cameras marketed in the United States, and these are adaptable to a variety of different customer requirements. Cameras can also be leased as needed, and every microfilm user can readily avail himself of the camera equipment at his local microfilm service company.

Summing up, it may be said that planetary cameras are needed for most precision microfilming jobs, such as the recording of engineering drawings, or in cases where documents are oversize or require special attention before filming to create an acceptable microfilm image.

Rotary cameras will prove satisfactory and speedy in applications where resolution and background density (degree of contrast between image and background) are not critical. This takes in a multitude of clerical operations in the microfilming of checks, receipts, purchase orders, and other business documents.

SYSTEMS ATTACHMENTS

Recently, manufacturers have developed accessory equipment for use with rotary cameras that will be of interest to records managers and systems analysts. Basically, these accessories are designed to add data to a record just prior to its microfilming. For example, sequential numbering accessory for use with a rotary microfilm camera may enter an identifying number on sales invoices that are microfilmed prior to mailing. Another accessory may be used to assign a file identification number to correspondence prior to microfilming. Still another may enter f.o.b. points on bills of lading.

Comprehensive but separate lists of both rotary and planetary cameras are given in Figs. 8–7 and 8–8. They include special characteristics and price ranges.

Chapter 9

Readers and Printers

The most common and important piece of apparatus to any user of microfilm is a reader. These can range from hand viewers, such as are used for occasional reading of micro-opaque cards and microfiche, to projectors designed for group viewing of an image projected on a large wall screen. But the latter is special equipment. Most microfilm is viewed from table readers that present a rear projection image on a viewing screen large enough to reproduce a legal-size document.

The operation of a microfilm reader is quite simple. In the case of roll microfilm, the film is unwound by means of a hand crank or motor that pulls successive film images past a beam of light. The beam of light forms an image after passing through the microfilm and lens. The image is positioned by one or more mirrors until it is imposed in magnified form on the translucent viewing screen. This form of projection provides an image bright enough to be read without darkening a room. In Fig. 9–6, all elements at the top of the machine are situated on a turntable or rotating head. This makes it possible to "turn" the image so that it will appear right side up on the screen even if not recorded that way on the film. The film is cranked forward or backward in searching a roll. When viewed, the film is held in proper relationship to the lens and light source by the glass flats. The mirror beneath the lens positions the image on the viewing screen.

Fig. 9–1. The Recordak "310" film reader is a low-cost machine for view-ing 16mm roll microfilm. A 9″ × 12″ screen is provided. The entire unit weighs 23 pounds and occupies about the same amount of desk space as a typewriter.

Fig. 9–2. The Film-A-Record reader is designed to accommodate 35mm roll microfilm, jacketed microfilm, or aperture cards. Large engineering drawings are reproduced on the 18″ × 24″ screen that is illuminated by a 500-watt projection lamp. This machine is manufactured by the Remington Office Systems Division of Sperry Rand Corporation.

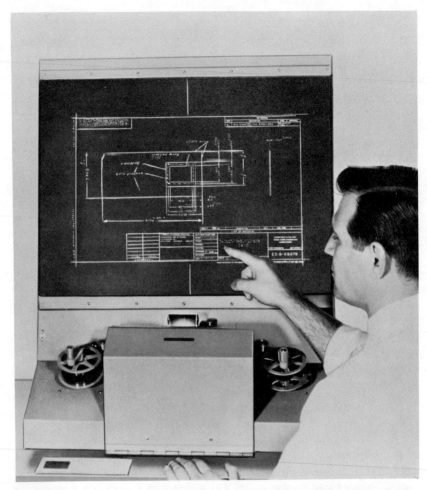

Fig. 9–3. The Recordak 1824 film reader (Model MK6) is designed for viewing large and very detailed engineering drawings by groups as well as individuals. It will magnify the entire frame area of a standard 35mm aperture card fifteen times without filling its screen area. The optical system incorporates a heat-absorbing filter and a motor-driven fan to dissipate heat from its 500-watt projection lamp. The screen is green tinted. This machine is designed to accommodate 35mm roll microfilm as well as aperture cards.

Fig. 9–4. The Recordak portable aperture card reader (Model MER) is a convenient reader for desk-top viewing of aperture cards. Magnification of the image on the 10½″ × 12″ screen is 15 to 1. The user views segments rather than the entire aperture card image. A lever allows him to scan the complete image in all directions. Weight is 31 pounds.

Fig. 9–5. All reading of microfilm need not be done in the office. This portable unit from Recordak can operate on its own battery, from a 12-volt automobile battery, or on 120-volt alternating current. Inside the storage case there is room for storing six 100-foot 16mm microfilm magazines. Such a device is valuable to engineers and technicians who may need to check references in the field, and also to salesmen making presentations on technical products.

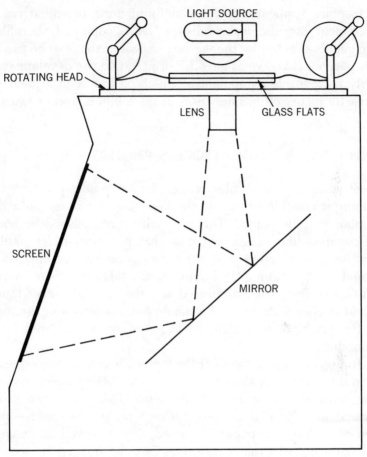

Fig. 9–6. Simplified diagram of microfilm reader.

In office applications, it is usually of great benefit if reading equipment can also make full-size "hard" copies of microfilmed documents selected by the viewer. A reader that can be used for this purpose is known as a reader-printer, and the development of fairly inexpensive equipment of this type has been a great spur to vastly increased business uses of microfilm in recent years.

SILVER-PROCESS PRINTERS

Expanding a microfilm reader into a reader-printer means making it possible to impose the enlarged film image on a sheet of photographic paper. This is usually accomplished by adding a simplified film developing unit that processes silver-emulsion printing paper. Such processing, occurring in a completely enclosed tray containing the liquid, usually takes less than a minute. An almost-dry print is delivered and the operator never touches liquid or chemicals, unless he should have to replenish the supply in the machine by adding packages or tubes prepared by the manufacturer.

In Fig. 9–7, all elements at the top of the machine are the same as in the diagram of the reader (Fig. 9–6). Differences start with the movable mirror beneath the lens. The image can first be viewed and then, if desired, focused on photo-sensitive paper beneath. After the paper is exposed, it is conveyed into a chemical bath or baths that develop and fix the image. In actuality, the process is, of course, considerably more complicated. There are a number of chemical and mechanical approaches to designing microfilm printers, and all of them do not rely on wet-process chemical baths.

The process, it will be noted, is similar to the operation of office photocopiers. The only important difference being that the image is imposed on the printing paper by projection of the microfilm, rather than by a contact printing process when an original document might be duplicated in a photocopier. Arrangement is usually made for projection printing by moving out of the way of the projection beam the mirror that ordinarily imposes the beam on the reader screen. Instead, the image is imposed on the printing paper. (See Figs. 9–8, 9–9, and 9–10.)

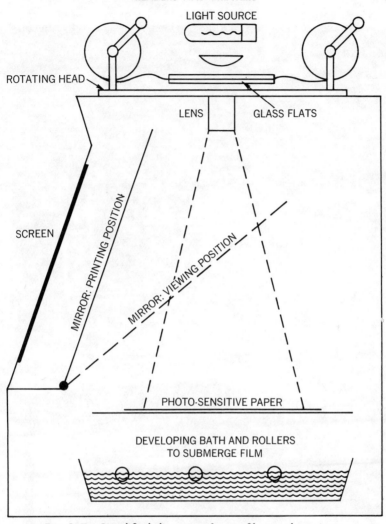

LIGHT SOURCE

ROTATING HEAD

LENS GLASS FLATS

SCREEN

MIRROR: PRINTING POSITION

MIRROR: VIEWING POSITION

PHOTO-SENSITIVE PAPER

DEVELOPING BATH AND ROLLERS
TO SUBMERGE FILM

Fig. 9–7. Simplified diagram of microfilm reader-printer.

Fig. 9–8. The Magnaprint reader-printer from Recordak (Model PE-14) is designed to accept a variety of microforms. The basic machine accommodates 16mm and 35mm roll microfilm. Accessory kits adapt it to accept film magazines, aperture cards, film jackets, and microfiche. Five interchangeable lenses are available to provide different magnifications. The viewing screen is 11 inches square and green tinted. Silver-process prints up to 8″ × 10″ are produced by this machine.

Fig. 9–9. The compact "Quadrant" printer from the 3M Company is a desk-top machine that makes 8½" × 11" prints on dry-process silver emulsion paper. Aperture cards are the input. Hard copies of a large engineering drawing are made by reproducing it in four quadrants.

Fig. 9–10. Itek "1824" reader-printer is a large-size version of the smaller silver-process microfilm reader-printers illustrated elsewhere in this book. Its systems applications are different, however, since it is well adapted to making readable prints of large-size engineering drawings. At the same time, it is capable of producing continuous-tone prints that will reproduce photographs clearly, something the Xerox 1824 printer cannot do as well.

ELECTROLYTIC METHOD

Other printing methods to obtain enlargements are also in wide use. The 3M Company's "Filmac" reader-printers employ an electrolytic form of development in which a printing paper coated with a thin metallic layer that is both light-sensitive and an electrical conductor is used. This makes it possible to develop a latent image by depositing silver dyes by electrolysis.

The "Filmac 400" reader-printer (Fig. 9–11) is designed for use as part of a simple office information retrieval system making use of 16mm roll microfilm contained in self-threading cartridges. The Filmac 400 system differs from the Recordak Lodestar system in that retrieval is accomplished by means of a counter on the machine. The operator watches the counter, which resets itself at zero when a new magazine is inserted, instead of the screen. The approximate number for locating any document is determined

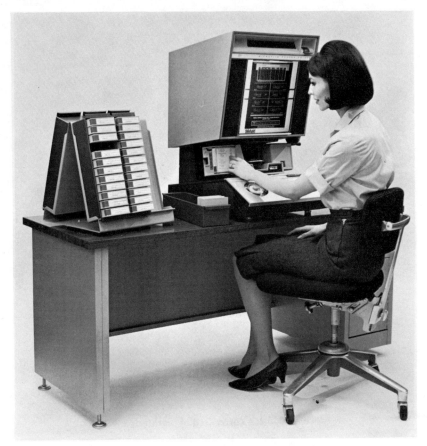

Fig. 9–11. Filmac 400 reader-printer.

from an index that is typed on the label of each cartridge. Other reader-printers in this group are designed to accept all varieties of microfilm *except* cartridges.

ELECTROSTATIC PRINTERS

For applications requiring large-size copies of engineering drawings, electrostatic printers such as the Xerox "1824" (Fig. 9–12) have come into wide use. As its name implies, this machine makes 18″ × 24″ hard copies from microfilm. Among its advantages are the fact that it can employ almost any kind of ordinary

Fig. 9–12. Xerox "1824" printer.

paper for copying, and that the process is fast and completely dry.

The principle on which electrostatic copying is based involves the action of light in forming a latent image composed of varying electrostatic charges on a selenium drum within the machine. The latent image of static electricity becomes visible when an inky powder is deposited on it that is attracted only to portions of the surface that represent the image. This image is transferred by contact from the drum to printing paper, and the powdered ink is fixed to the paper by heat. In its actuality, the electrostatic process described here in very general terms is more complicated, as anyone who has ever examined the inside of a Xerox copier can testify.

The above method of electrostatic printing is known as transfer Xerography. The image is transferred from a drum to the printing paper. There is another electrostatic process known as the direct method. Here the printing paper is coated with metallic oxides that pick up the electrostatic charges that compose the latent image. This image is also developed by the deposit of powders and fixed by heat.

DIAZO PRINTERS

A final printing method used in making enlargements from microfilm is the diazo process. In this case, the microfilm image is projected on diazo paper and developed in the same manner as white prints are made in the diazo machines common to engineering drafting facilities. The diazo paper is coated with diazonium salts that react to ultraviolet light, becoming colorless. A latent image is created during projection on the portion of the paper that light does not strike. The paper then passes through an alkaline developing bath in which the diazo salts in the latent image areas are converted to an azo dye that becomes the permanent image.

VOLUME PRODUCTION

Most available reader-printers and enlarging printers are designed to produce one or a few copies as needed; but, for systems applications requiring a large volume of copies of a single drawing, or varying number of copies of successive drawings, there is also equipment available capable of producing varying numbers of copies directly from microfilm. These employ either the electrostatic method or a variation of the silver printing paper method. Machines such as the Xerox "Copyflo" are well adapted to producing volume orders of both engineering drawings and smaller documents (Fig. 9–13). Its output, usually needed only at large facilities or service bureaus, is 20 linear feet per minute. The continuous sheet it delivers is 24 inches wide.

A number of wet-process machines using long rolls of silver emulsion photographic paper are useful in filling large orders for record duplication at high speed. The latter was the method used

Fig. 9–13. Xerox Copyflo continuous printer.

for making the printout of the World War II V-Mail. Because of their high price, these complex machines are more likely to be rented than purchased, as are computers and other data processing hardware. In applications where such equipment is needed only infrequently, a microfilm service bureau can usually fill a company's needs. Also, it is well to remember that offset masters can be generated from microfilm. Once this is done, requirements for duplication jobs, such as making 1,000 copies of a brochure contained on a microfiche transparency, can be handled by any offset duplicator.

This chapter ends with an extensive list of microfilm readers and reader-printers inclusive enough to satisfy most needs (Figs. 9–14 and 9–15 *). The primary breakdown is by price, so that the records manager will have an easier time staying within his budget. This should make it more simple to locate equipment

* See pages 108–127.

listings capable of satisfying his requirements at the most reasonable price. However, it is well to remember that the cheapest equipment is not always the best in the long run, particularly if heavy use is anticipated. Further, there are very handy features, such as the ability of a reader to rotate images, that are not included in all lower-priced machines. Microfilm images may sometimes be printed with reading material running vertically as well as horizontally on microfilm. The image rotation feature enables the viewer to read a normal image with horizontal lines of information even if the image is not printed that way on the film.

HAND VIEWERS

Hand microfilm readers are not included in the detailed listings because they rightfully belong in a separate category. There are a large number of pocket magnifiers available that can be used by a man in the field to provide on-the-spot views of the contents of a microfilm. Such viewers are, of course, not satisfactory for extensive study of microfilmed information, but they are economical. Their magnification powers range from $3\times$ up to about $20\times$, depending on the product. Basically, most are not unlike the pocket magnifiers often called thread counters used in the textile and printing trades. Some models provide their own illumination from small battery-powered lamps. Manufacturers include the 3M Company, Microcard Corporation, Optics Manufacturing Corporation, and the Taylor-Merchant Corporation.

Price Range	Manufacturer	Model	Type of Microform Accepted
A. Under $124.99	Camera Optics	Micro-Reader	a. 35mm aperture cards
	Keuffel & Esser Co. (K & E)	Viewer-Scanner	a. 105mm sheet film
	Microdealers	Draftsman 708 Big R	a. 16mm roll film
		Draftsman 708B	a. 35mm aperture cards
B. $125.00 to $199.99	Atlantic Microfilm	MJR-85	a. All 16mm micro-forms except micro opaques b. All 35mm micro-forms except micro-opaques
	Documentation, Inc.	1010 Reader	a. Roll film b. Microfiche c. Aperture cards
	Dukane	576-95	a. Microfiche
		576-70	a. 35mm aperture cards
	Eugene Dietzgen	4305	a. 35mm aperture cards
	Federal Division of Victoreen Instrument Co.	701	a. All 16mm micro-forms except micro-opaques b. All 35mm micro-forms except micro-opaques
	General Aniline and Film	5685	a. All 16mm micro-forms except micro-opaques b. All 35mm micro-forms except micro-opaques
	Keuffel & Esser Co. (K & E)	Micromaster 35	a. 16mm aperture cards b. 35mm aperture cards
		Microfiche V.S.	a. Microfiche
	Microcard Corp.	FR-5 Reader	a. 16mm acetate jackets b. 16mm microfiche
	Microdealers	Draftsman 708C	a. 35mm roll film b. 35mm aperture cards

Fig. 9–14. Classified directory

Viewing Screen Area	Magnification Area	Accessories and Features	Image Rotation
10″ × 13″	10×	Manually operated.	No
4″ × 6″	3×	Manually operated.	No
10″ × 13″	20×	Manually operated.	No
10″ × 13″	10×	Manually operated.	No
10″ × 10″	11× 15× 22×	Manually operated. May be adapted to accept roll film.	No
10″ × 10″	18× to 24×	Manually operated.	Yes
10½″ × 12″	15×	Manually operated.	No
10½″ × 12″	15×	Manually operated.	No
10½″ × 12″	14.75×	Manually operated.	No
Projects variable-size image on screen.	6× to 60×	Manually operated.	Yes
10″ × 10″	11× 22×	Manually operated.	Yes
10½″ × 12″	15×	Manually operated.	No
10½″ × 12″	15×	Manually operated.	No
7½″ × 9½″	16½×	Manually operated. Integral indexing system available.	No
12″ × 18″	12×	Manually operated. Roll film attachment available.	No

of microfilm readers.

Price Range	Manufacturer	Model	Type of Microform Accepted
B. $125.00 to $199.99 (cont'd)	Remington Office Systems Division of Sperry Rand Corp.	F-440	a. 16mm aperture cards b. 35mm aperture cards
C. $200.00 to $350.00	Atlantic Microfilm	MF-46	a. Microfiche in 4″ × 6″ format
	Bell & Howell Co.	BH-206	a. 16mm roll film b. 35mm roll film
	Documat	F	a. 16mm roll film, acetate jackets, and aperture cards b. 35mm roll film, acetate jackets, and aperture cards
	Dukane	576-75	a. Microfiche
		576-80	a. 16mm roll film and aperture cards b. 35mm roll film and aperture cards
	Eugene Dietzgen	4314	a. 35mm aperture cards
		4312	a. 16mm acetate jackets b. 16mm aperture cards c. 35mm acetate jackets d. 35mm aperture cards
		4307	a. 16mm roll film b. 35mm roll film
		4305-20	a. 35mm aperture cards
		4308	a. 16mm roll film
	IBM Corp.	Micro-Viewer	a. 16mm roll film and aperture cards b. 35mm roll film and aperture cards
	Itek Business Products	12 × 12 Reader	a. 16mm roll film

Fig. 9–14.

Viewing Screen Area	Magnification Area	Accessories and Features	Image Rotation
10½″ × 12″	15×	Manually operated.	No
11″ × 14″	24×	Manually operated.	No
8″ × 10″	24× to 37×	Manually operated. Has scanning ability. Uses indexing system using 1,000 locator points per 100 feet.	Yes
11″ × 11″	15× 24× 35×	Manually operated.	Yes
11″ × 14″	24×	Manually operated.	No
10½″ × 12″	15×	Manually operated.	Yes
10½″ × 12″	15×	Manually operated.	No
12″ × 12″	17× 24× 30× 43×	Manually operated.	No
14″ × 14″	17× 23× 30× 43×	Manually operated.	Yes
10½″ × 12″	20×	Manually operated.	No
12″ × 12″	17× 24× 30× 43×	Manually operated.	Yes
8″ × 10″	6.5×	Manually operated.	Yes
12″ × 12″	24×	Manually operated.	Yes

Continued.

Price Range	Manufacturer	Model	Type of Microform Accepted
C. $200.00 to $350.00 (cont'd)	Microcard Corp.	Micro III	a. All 16mm micro forms except aperture cards
		Mark IV Reader	a. 16mm microfiche
	Recordak Corp.	PFC-58	a. 16mm microfiche and acetate jackets b. 35mm microfiche and acetate jackets
		PFC-46-1	a. 16mm microfiche and acetate jackets b. 35mm microfiche and acetate jackets
		MKR-1	a. 35mm aperture cards
	Remington Office Systems Division of Sperry Rand Corp.	Film-A-Record Reader	a. 16mm roll film b. 35mm roll film
		Kard-A-Film Reader	a. All 16mm micro-forms b. All 35mm micro-forms
		Series 420	a. All 16mm micro-forms b. All 35mm micro-forms
D. Over $350.00	Documat	U	a. All 16mm micro-forms b. All 35mm micro-forms
		D	a. 16mm roll film, acetate jackets, and aperture cards b. 35mm roll film, acetate jackets, and aperture cards
		R	a. 16mm roll film b. 35mm roll film
		200Z	a. All 16mm micro-forms except micro-opaques b. All 35mm micro-forms except micro-opaques

Fig. 9–14.

Viewing Screen Area	Magnification Area	Accessories and Features	Image Rotation
8″ × 9½″	19×	Manually operated.	Yes
9½″ × 11″	18×	Manually operated.	Yes
10½″ × 13¼″	18× to 26.5×	Manually operated. Vertical alphabetical scale used as integral indexing system.	No
10½″ × 13¼″	18× to 26.4×	Manually operated.	No
10½″ × 12″	15×	Manually operated. Has scanning ability.	No
14″ × 14″	17× 23× 30× 43×	Manually operated. Has scanning ability.	Yes
12″ × 12″	24×	Manually operated.	Yes
11″ × 11″	15× 24× 35×	Manually operated. Has scanning ability.	Yes
11″ × 11″	15× 25× 35×	Manually operated. Has scanning ability.	Yes
11″ × 11″	15× 25× 35×	Manually operated. Has scanning ability.	Yes
11″ × 11″	15× 25× 35×	Manually operated. Has scanning ability.	Yes
11″ × 11″	15× 25× 35×	Manually operated. Has scanning ability.	Yes

Continued.

Price Range	Manufacturer	Model	Type of Microform Accepted
D. Over $350.00 (cont'd)	Documat (cont'd)	200Z (cont'd)	c. All 70mm and 105mm microforms except micro-opaques
		200M	a. All 16mm micro-forms except micro-opaques b. All 35mm micro-forms except micro-opaques c. All 70mm and 105mm microforms except micro-opaques
	Eugene Dietzgen	4313	a. 16mm roll film and aperture cards b. 35mm roll film and aperture cards
	Keuffel & Esser Co. (K & E)	105M Viewer	a. 105mm sheet film
	Microcard Corp.	Mark VII	a. 16mm micro-opaques
	Microdealers	Draftsman 708D	a. 35mm roll film and aperture cards
	Microseal Corp.	U2-F and U2-B	a. 16mm aperture cards b. 35mm aperture cards
	Recordak Corp.	PK-1013	a. 16mm microfiche and acetate jackets b. 35mm microfiche and acetate jackets
		MPE-1	a. 16mm roll film b. 35mm roll film
		PTA	a. 16mm roll film b. 16mm roll film in magazines
		1824	a. 35mm roll film and aperture cards
		PV and PVA	a. 16mm roll film
		P-20	a. 16mm roll film b. 16mm roll film in magazines

Fig. 9–14.

Viewing Screen Area	Magnification Area	Accessories and Features	Image Rotation
11″ × 11″	15×	Motor driven. Has scanning ability.	Yes
18″ × 24″	14.75×	Manually operated. Has scanning ability.	Yes
16″ × 24″	4×	Manually operated.	Yes
9⅞″ × 10½″	21×	Manually operated.	No
18″ × 24″	15×	Manually operated.	No
18″ × 24″	14×	Manually operated.	No
10½″ × 13¼″	18× 23×	Manually operated. Lenses are interchangeable.	No
20″ × 20″	19×	Manually operated. Has scanning ability.	Yes
10⅝″ × 12″	20×	Motor driven. Has code scale capable of providing integral indexing.	No
18″ × 24″	15×	Manually operated. Has scanning ability.	No
9″ × 12″	20× 24× 32× 40×	Manually operated. Has scanning ability. Interchangeable lenses available.	Yes
9″ × 12″	20×	Motor driven. Has scanning ability. Has code scale capable of providing integral indexing.	No

Continued.

115

Price Range	Manufacturer	Model	Type of Microform Accepted
D. Over $350.00 (cont'd)	Remington Office Systems Division of Sperry Rand Corp.	F-478	a. 16mm roll film, acetate jackets, and aperture cards b. 35mm roll film, acetate jackets, and aperture cards
		AO	a. 16mm roll film b. 35mm roll film
		F-458	a. Aperture cards b. Acetate jackets c. Microfiche

Fig. 9–14.

Price Range	Manufacturer	Model	Types of Microforms Accepted	Viewing Screen Area	Magnification Ratio
A. Under $500.00	Documentation, Inc.	Mark 5 Printer	a. 16mm roll film b. Aperture cards c. Acetate jackets d. Microfiche	10″ × 8″	18× to 24×
	Federal Division of Victoreen Instrument Co.	Micromate	a. 16 mm and 35 mm roll film b. Aperture cards c. Acetate jackets d. Microfiche	8″ × 10″ to 18″ × 24″	6× to 16½×
		473	a. 16mm roll film b. Aperture cards c. Acetate jackets d. Microfiche	8″ × 9½″	18.5×
	Keuffel & Esser Co. (K & E)	52-2014	a. 105mm roll film	12″ × 18″	3×

Fig. 9–15. Classified directory

Viewing Screen Area	Magnification Area	Accessories and Features	Image Rotation
18″ × 24″	14.75×	Manually operated. Has scanning ability.	Yes
14½″ × 14½″	23× 40×	Motor driven. Has scanning ability. Equipped with foot switch.	Yes
12″ × 12″	24×	Manually operated.	No

Concluded.

Print Size	Copies May Be Produced on:	No. of Prints per Min.	Cost per Print	Accessories and Fixtures	Image Rotation
8″ × 10″	Sensitized paper	1	6¢	Manually operated. Coin actuation attachment available. Interchangeable lenses.	Yes
8″ × 10″ to 12″ × 18″	Sensitized paper and transparencies	4 to 12 (depending upon size)	6¢ to 14¢ (depending upon size)	Manually operated. Uses pre-cut sheets. Available with 18″ processor.	Yes
8″ × 9½″	Sensitized paper and transparencies	5 to 12 (depending upon processing method)	5¢ to 7¢ (depending upon size)	Manually operated. Uses pre-cut sheets. Prints may be prepared by either diffusion transfer or stabilization process.	Yes
12″ × 18″	Sensitized paper	2	20¢	Manually operated.	No

of reader-printers.

117

Price Range	Manufacturer	Model	Types of Microforms Accepted	Viewing Screen Area	Magnification Ratio
B. $500.00 to $799.99	Keuffel & Esser Co. (K & E)	52-3021	a. 105mm sheet film	16″ × 24″	4×
		35mm Pedestel 52-2033	a. 35mm roll film b. Aperture cards	18″ × 24″	14.5×
		35mm	a. 35mm roll film b. Aperture cards	18″ × 24″	14.5×
C. $800.00 to $999.99	Bell & Howell Co.	530D	a. 16mm and 35mm roll film b. Aperture cards c. Acetate jackets d. Microfiche	11″ × 11″	10.5× to 37×
	Documat, Inc.	300Z	a. Roll film from 16mm through 105mm (using roll film adapter) b. Aperture cards c. Acetate jackets d. Microfiche e. Film strips	11″ × 11″	10.5× 13.4× 20.1× 27.9× 33.8×
		Mark II	a. 16mm and 35mm roll film b. Aperture cards c. Acetate jackets	11″ × 11″	10.5× 13.4× 20.1× 27.9× 33.8×
	3M Co.	Filmac 100	a. 16mm and 35mm roll film b. Aperture cards c. Acetate jackets d. Microfiche	7¼″ × 8½″	7× to 26×

Fig. 9–15.

Print Size	Copies May Be Produced on:	No. of Prints per Min.	Cost per Print	Accessories and Fixtures	Image Rotation
16″ × 24″	Sensitized paper	2	25¢	Manually operated. Sheet fed.	No
18″ × 24″	Sensitized paper	2	25¢	Manually operated. Sheet fed.	No
18″ × 24″	Sensitized paper	2	25¢	Available either as manually operated or motor driven. Sheet fed.	No
8½″ × 11″	Sensitized paper	2	8¢	Manually operated. Has scanning ability. Integral indexing system with 1,000 reference points per 100 feet is standard.	Yes
8½″ × 11″ (actual image area is 7″ × 9¼″)	Sensitized paper	2	8¢	Manually operated. Has scanning ability. Paper is automatically cut and trimmed from roll as prints are produced. Interchangeable lenses.	Yes
8½″ × 11″ (actual image area is 7″ × 9¼″)	Sensitized paper	2	8¢	Manually operated. Has scanning ability.	Yes
8¼″ × 11″	Sensitized paper	6	8¢	Available either as manually operated or motor driven. Microfiche attachment available.	Yes

Continued.

Price Range	Manufacturer	Model	Types of Microforms Accepted	Viewing Screen Area	Magnification Ratio
C. $800.00 to $999.99 (cont'd)	Remington Office Systems Division of Sperry Rand Corp.	F-468	a. 16mm and 35mm roll film b. Aperture cards c. Acetate jackets d. Microfiche	11" × 11"	16× to 42×
D. $1,000.00 to $1,499.99	Documat, Inc.	300M	a. 16mm through 105mm roll film (using roll film adapter) b. Aperture cards c. Acetate jackets d. Microfiche e. Film strips	11" × 11"	10.5× 13.4× 20.1× 27.9× 33.8×
		300A	a. 16mm through 105mm roll film (using roll film adapter) b. Aperture cards c. Acetate jackets d. Microfiche e. Film strips	11" × 11"	10.5× 13.4× 20.1× 27.9× 33.8×
	Keuffel & Esser Co. (K & E)	52-2006	a. 105mm sheet film	16" × 24"	4×
	3M Co.	Filmac 200	a. 16mm and 35mm roll film b. Aperture cards c. Acetate jackets	18" × 24"	14.5×
	Poly Repro International	M-16A	a. 16mm and 35mm roll film b. Aperture cards c. Acetate jackets d. Microfiche	8½" × 14"	11× to 36×

Fig. 9–15.

Print Size	Copies May Be Produced on:	No. of Prints per Min.	Cost per Print	Accessories and Fixtures	Image Rotation
8½″ × 11″	Sensitized paper	4	8¢	Manually operated.	Yes
8½″ × 11″ (actual image area is 7″ × 9¼″)	Sensitized paper	2	8¢	Motor driven. Has scanning ability. Paper is automatically cut from roll and trimmed as prints are produced. Interchangeable lenses.	Yes
8½″ × 11″ (actual image area is 7″ × 9¼″)	Sensitized paper	2	8¢	Motor driven. Has automatic step and print feature. Paper is automatically cut from roll and trimmed as prints are produced. Interchangeable lenses.	Yes
16″ × 24″	Sensitized paper	2	25¢	Manually operated.	No
18″ × 24″	Sensitized paper	3	8¢	Manually operated.	Yes
8½″ × 14″	Sensitized paper and offset mats	2	9¢	Motor driven.	Yes

Continued.

Price Range	Manufacturer	Model	Types of Microforms Accepted	Viewing Screen Area	Magnifi- cation Ratio
D. $1,000.00 to $1,499.99 (cont'd)	Recordak Corp.	PE-1A	a. 16mm and 35mm roll film b. Aperture cards c. Acetate jackets d. Microfiche	11″ × 11″	11.8× to 38×
E. Over $1,500.00	Bell & Howell Co.	Autoload	a. 16mm roll film in cartridges	14″ × 14″	20.1× 40.1×
	General Aniline and Film	Microline	a. 16mm and 35mm roll film b. Aperture cards c. Acetate jackets d. Micro- opaques e. Microfiche	18″ × 24″	14.7×
	Itek Business Products	1824 Reader- Printer	a. 16mm and 35mm roll film b. Aperture cards c. Acetate jackets d. Microfiche	18″ × 24″	14.7×
	3M Co.	Filmac 300	a. 16mm and 35mm roll film b. Aperture cards c. Acetate jackets d. Microfiche	11″ × 14″	7× to 20×

Fig. 9–15.

Print Size	Copies May Be Produced on:	No. of Prints per Min.	Cost per Print	Accessories and Fixtures	Image Rotation
8.1" × 10.1"	Sensitized paper	2.3	8¢	Motor driven. Has code scale as integral indexing system.	Yes
8½" × 11"	Sensitized paper	2	8¢	Motor driven. Has scanning ability. Duel magnification available through zoom lens.	Yes
Up to 18" × 24"	Sensitized paper and translucent paper	Varies according to size of print	Varies according to size of print	Manually operated. Stacker module attachment. Print size may be adjusted to provide copies from 8½" × 11" up to 18" × 24". When less than 18" × 24" print is to be produced, the unwanted area is masked on both the viewing screen and the print material.	No
Up to 18" × 24"	Sensitized paper, translucent paper, and offset mats	2	Varies according to size of print	Manually operated. Selective masking to make prints of small areas of drawing.	No
11" × 4" to 11" × 14"	Sensitized paper	6	8¢	Manually operated.	Yes

Continued.

Price Range	Manufacturer	Model	Types of Microforms Accepted	Viewing Screen Area	Magnification Ratio
E. Over $1,500.00 (cont'd)	3M Co. (cont'd)	Filmac 400	a. 16mm and 35mm roll film b. 16mm roll film in cartridges c. Aperture cards d. Acetate jackets e. Microfiche	10" × 11½"	10.6× to 29×
		111 Dry Silver Printer	a. Aperture cards	None	12.6× or 14.25×
	Poly Repro International	M-35	a. Aperture cards	18" × 24"	13× to 16.5×
	Recordak Corp.	PES	a. 16mm roll film in magazines	13" × 13"	23×
		P-1824	a. 35mm roll film b. Aperture cards c. Acetate jackets d. Microfiche	18" × 24"	14.7×
	Xerox Corp.	1824	a. 16mm and 35mm roll film b. Aperture cards c. Acetate jackets d. Microfiche	5" × 6"	14.5×
		Copyflo 24C	a. Aperture cards	None	15× 20×

Fig. 9–15.

Print Size	Copies May Be Produced on:	No. of Prints per Min.	Cost per Print	Accessories and Fixtures	Image Rotation
8¼″ × 12½″	Sensitized paper	12	8¢	Motor driven.	Yes
8½″ × 11″	Sensitized paper	5 to 7	2¢	Manually operated. Dry silver copies. Conversion kit available.	No
18″ × 24″	Sensitized paper and offset mats	2	24¢	Manually operated.	No
8½″ × 11″	Sensitized paper	2.3	8¢	Motor driven. Automatic.	No
18″ × 24″	Sensitized paper	2	24¢	Available either as motor driven or manually operated.	No
8½″ × 11″ to 18″ × 24″	Ordinary paper, translucent paper, and offset mats	2 to 3 (depending upon size)	Varies according to print media used	Manually operated. Usually leased.	No
Up to 24″ × any variable length	Ordinary paper, translucent paper, and offset mats	20 linear feet per minute	Varies according to print media used	Motor driven. Usually leased.	No

Continued.

Price Range	Manufacturer	Model	Types of Microforms Accepted	Viewing Screen Area	Magnifi- cation Ratio
E. Over $1,500.00 (cont'd)	Xerox Corp. (cont'd)	Copyflo 11	a. 16mm and 35mm roll film	None	7× to 24×

Fig. 9–15.

EQUIPMENT NEEDS

The foregoing tables show that there is a wide variety of microfilm readers and reader-printers available to meet almost any kind of system's need.

Generally speaking, the equipment requirements for the average company's microfilm facility are not heavy. Reader-printers and storage facilities for the film are usually the only basic needs. Camera work can be handled by a service company if so desired.

Obviously, a single reader-printer convenient to the storage area is all that is required in the case of a repository of aging records maintained mostly for legal purposes. However, in the case of active sales, engineering, or research documents, the situation is different and should be carefully examined by the records manager and systems analyst. The time wasted by employees standing in line to make enlarged copies of microfilm and the irritation generated can dissipate the savings and destroy the efficiency one has the right to expect from a well-conceived microfilm system.

Consider the case of an eastern chemical company where abstracts of reports on worldwide research were put on 16mm roll microfilm. It was found that heavy reference demands created bottlenecks at the single reader-printer allocated. It was also determined that additional reader-printers would not solve the problem completely because a number of people were frequently waiting to examine the same cartridge of 16mm film.

Print Size	Copies May Be Produced on:	No. of Prints per Min.	Cost per Print	Accessories and Fixtures	Image Rotation
11″ × any variable length	Ordinary paper, translucent paper, and offset mats	20 linear feet per minute	Varies according to print media used	Motor driven. Automatic cutter that trims prints as they emerge is optional. Usually leased.	No

Concluded.

Not only additional reader-printers but duplicate film would be needed to set the situation right.

Consideration is being given at the time of this writing to a hybrid system whereby bound volumes of the original abstracts would be maintained as a file for general reference on a first-come, first-served basis, while, at the same time, use of the microfilm would be restricted to a relatively small group of literature searchers whose work is most important to the company. These individuals would be able to quickly search the microfilm files and print out copies of needed information.

This is not a completely satisfactory solution, but one dictated by cost factors. When funds are budgeted to expand the system, presumably it will go all-microfilm.

An important point to remember when selecting readers and printers is that, while one reader capable of accepting, say, 16mm film is to that extent compatible with any other 16mm reader, the roll film cartridges and coding methods associated with popular indexing systems are not usually compatible with different machines. One cannot arbitrarily mix machines of various manufacturers.

Emphasis should constantly be placed on the need for careful planning in the setting up of a microfilm system so that it will really do its job in facilitating reference and cutting document storage costs.

Chapter 10

Processing Equipment

Although the great majority of users return their exposed microfilm to the manufacturer for processing, there are instances in which it may be desirable for the user to establish and operate his own microfilm processing laboratory. In such instances, you will find one or more of the following factors involved.

1. *Distance from the nearest microfilm processing laboratory.* The user may be located a considerable distance from the nearest microfilm processing laboratory. Rather than endure the additional cost, risk and delay of mailing his microfilm to a distant city, and the inconvenience of waiting several days for its return, he may decide to install his own processing equipment.

2. *There is a need for absolute control over the microfilm.* A user may microfilm records that, to protect his proprietary interests, must be guarded against loss, theft, or unauthorized disclosure. While the chances of such loss, theft, or unauthorized disclosure are very small in using a reputable outside processing laboratory, the user may feel safer if certain types of records and the microfilms of those records remain in the hands of his personnel at all times. Therefore, he may decide to process his own microfilm, even though the cost of doing so may be higher than using the manufacturer's processing laboratory.

3. *A heavy volume of microfilm is processed.* Raw microfilm is sold either with the price of processing included in the sales

price or with the price of processing in addition to the sales price. It varies according to the manufacturer; but, generally, the cost of microfilm sold with processing included will be $1.00 or more per roll higher than the price of microfilm with processing extra.

If a company films several thousand microfilm rolls annually, and anticipates continuing this level in the future, it will probably be more economical for them to purchase the necessary equipment and train their personnel to process their own microfilm than to continue using an outside processing laboratory.

4. *The microfilm is an important link in a systems cycle.* Many systems provide that, at some point during the systems cycle, records will be microfilmed. Frequently, it will be necessary for the user to determine that the microfilm is of acceptable quality before the systems cycle can continue. An example of such a situation might be the case of a retailer who returns his customers' charge slips to them as a back-up for their monthly accounts receivable statement. Since the charge slips will pass out of the retailer's possession, it will be necessary for him to assure that the microfilm copies of the charge slips are acceptable before mailing the customer's statement. Since a delay will occur if the retailer mails his exposed microfilm to a service company laboratory for processing, he may instead install his own processing equipment, thereby reducing to a minimum the time it takes to process the microfilm.

The records manager of a company that needs to process its own microfilm will find that there are compact automatic processing machines on the market that operate under normal room lighting, eliminating the need for photographic darkrooms, open tanks, and similar equipment associated with photographic processing.

The Unipro processor (Fig. 10–1) from Remington Rand Office Systems is a reasonably compact unit that does all jobs connected with the processing of 16mm, 35mm, or 70mm roll microfilm. The operator's hands never come in contact with the developing solutions, and as many as twenty rolls of 35mm film can be developed by one tank filling.

A machine such as the recently marketed Recordak "Prostar" (Fig. 10–2) is a tabletop unit designed for both 16mm and 35mm roll microfilm that takes up only about 2 square feet of space. It requires little training to operate and will process lengths of film from 2 to 100 feet in length. Processed film begins to emerge about two minutes after insertion at the rate of 5 feet per minute. The machine's only needs in addition to electrical current are water supply and a drain. Premixed processing chemicals are supplied in disposable containers to simplify office use.

Fig. 10–1. Unipro automatic daylight film processor.

Listed below are some of the readily available microfilm processors suitable for the average in-plant installation handling 16mm or 35mm film, or both. Each of these processors is priced between $3,000 and $4,500, is simple to set up and operate, and has a low frequency of repair. Since there are so many variables to consider when evaluating microfilm processors, no attempt has been made to tabulate all the various features.

Manufacturer	Model	Capacity (feet)	Processing Speed (feet per minute)
Allen Products, Inc.	20M	400	20
Bell & Howell Co.	Specialist	400	18
Itek Corp.	UT-35-5	100	20
Keuffel & Esser Co.	52-2050	100	20
Microdealers, Inc.	Filmflow	100	5
3M Co.	Sepratron	1,200	12
Recordak Corp.	Prostar	100	5
Sperry Rand Corp.	Unipro	100	4

Fig. 10–2. Recordak "Prostar" film processor.

When microfilms of engineering drawings are processed within a company, additional specialized equipment will be needed if the quality of the microfilm is to be checked for conformity with the Department of Defense Specifications provided for in government contracts. This means that specific test targets filmed along with current work must be examined under a microscope for quality of resolution and the film tested frequently with a densitometer to determine if images have sufficient contrast to meet government standards. Such equipment is not particularly expensive, but maintaining the trained personnel to use it will prove a burden unless considerations of volume and speed justify the cost.

Other specialized equipment may be needed at installations where microfilm aperture cards are made from engineering drawings. These include precision devices for mounting the film in the various types of aperture cards available. All microfilm facilities will have at least occasional need for hand rewinds and splicers for checking and repairing role microfilm (Fig. 10–3).

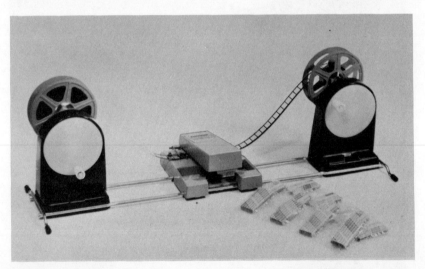

Fig. 10–3. The 16mm splicer and rewind combination is designed to handle non-perforated microfilm, but is in other ways similar to equipment used for motion picture film. The packages of splicing tape at lower right are made of extremely thin mylar film with a pressure adhesive coating. When the film is registered in the splicer, the tape is fixed to front and back.

DUPLICATING MICROFILM

In many applications, there is a need to make duplicates of entire rolls of microfilm. Various machines produce duplicate rolls on either silver diazo or Kalvar film. Clerical or reproduction department personnel can usually be trained to operate this equipment. Also available are a number of desk-top devices for making duplicate aperture cards. These devices are very easy to operate and serve a number of systems purposes. Duplicates can

Fig. 10–4. This compact unit from the 3M Company is known as the "Filmsort Uniprinter 086 Copier." It can deliver as many as 350 duplicate aperture cards per hour when operated at top speed. The image is copied and developed on diazo film.

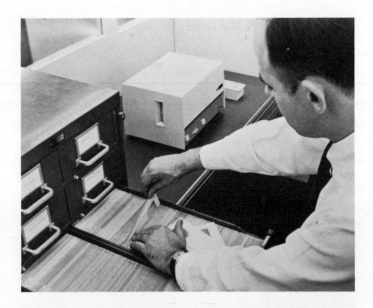

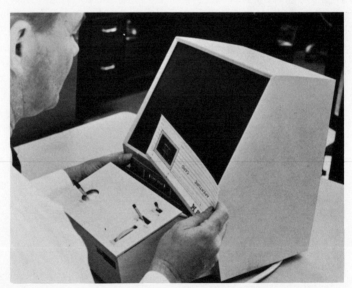

Fig. 10–5. In a system designed by IBM, duplicate aperture cards rather than enlarged prints from microfilm are used by engineers for checking purposes. The card is withdrawn from a file (*upper left*) and then inserted in a desk-top device (*upper right*) that makes a duplicate card by the Kalvar

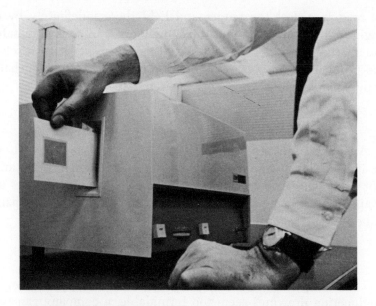

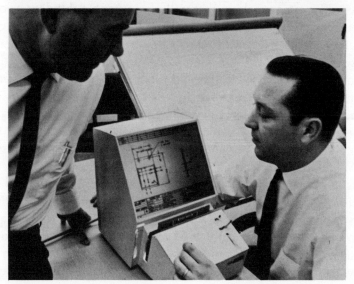

(ultraviolet light exposure) process. The original card can then be returned to preserve the integrity of the master file. The engineer examines the duplicate in a desk-top reader, and he can also hold it in a personal file.

be read in a desk-top reader and held there indefinitely by an engineer without disturbing the completeness of central or satellite aperture card files. A feature of this approach is that it solves the problem of reference without the necessity of making hardcopy enlargements. (See Figs. 10–4 and 10–5.)

APERTURE CARDS

Aperture cards are usually obtained already cut and with adhesive or a transparent envelope already mounted in a cutout area. For companies that use cards with sufficient volume, devices are available for cutting apertures in standard tabulating cards, fixing adhesive, and mounting the film.

AUTOMATIC CAMERA-PROCESSOR

If the requirements of in-company filming and processing of engineering drawings seem too formidable, a company can turn to an office-type machine that will photograph a drawing or other document and automatically deliver a finished aperture card without fuss. This machine is the "Filmsort 2000" camera-processor manufactured by the 3M Company (Fig. 10–6). It films documents up to 24″ × 36″ in size and produces a processed film image mounted in an aperture card in less than a minute. Use of such a machine allows a busy office to bypass the customary and sometimes slow process of batching such documents for filming by a planetary camera and then sending out the film for processing.

While such a machine cannot guarantee the precision results possible with trained personnel at planetary cameras and film processors, it provides a very convenient method of getting drawings immediately into files without waiting for a service company to process and mount batches of roll film. If the strictest quality controls need to be maintained, the drawings processed in this way can later be refilmed with regular batches under careful control.

FILING EQUIPMENT

There is also the problem of how microfilm will be stored. As will be discussed in more detail in Chapter 12, temperature and humidity conditions in the average air-conditioned office are

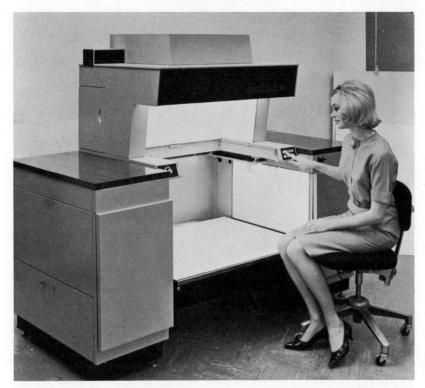

Fig. 10–6. Automatic microfilm camera processor ("Filmsort 2000").

reasonably well adapted to the preservation of microfilm images over the life span of the average business record. In cases where archival quality needs to be maintained, more rigid storage conditions are indicated, and these are also discussed in that chapter.

The user of microfilmed aperture cards will find that there is available to suit his needs a vast array of both simple and imaginatively designed filing equipment for tabulating cards. He can choose anywhere between small tub files and large-capacity motorized files that move trays of cards into access position on a conveyor belt at the touch of a button. This is quick-access equipment. Conventional file cabinets designed for tabulating cards are also widely marketed. Equally available are convenient file cabinets designed to hold the rolls of 16mm film and 16mm film magazines so widely used in office systems.

Chapter 11

Types of Microfilm Stock

Three very different types of film are now commonly used in microfilm applications. These are (1) standard silver nitrate photographic film stock, (2) diazo film, and (3) "Kalvar" (vesicular) film stock that permits development of the image by heat alone. Silver film is almost always used in making an original microfilm. The other two processes offer advantages in many applications involving the making of *duplicate* microfilms from a microfilm print. However, silver nitrate film stocks are widely used for this purpose also.

SILVER EMULSION FILM

We will discuss silver emulsion film first. This is the same type of emulsion that is used in the manufacture of films for all the varied photographic applications from the efforts of the amateur photographer to the making of printing masters for offset duplicators. The chemical composition of silver emulsion film is always basically the same, but the speed, or sensitivity of the emulsion, and its sensitivity to particular colors making up the spectrum of visible light may vary according to the purpose for which a particular film stock was designed. Silver films can be fast (extra sensitive) or slow (less sensitive but capable of producing a fine-grain image). They can be panchromatic (capable of showing gray scale variations for all the colors in the visible spectrum), or they can be particularly sensitive to one color, such as blue, and relatively insensitive to the other primary colors.

Panchromatic film is usually employed in microfilm cameras for photographing the original image, since it is more sensitive to all color variations in an image. Its wide response to color also permits photographic approaches whereby *unwanted* tints or discolorations can be eliminated from the film image by blocking them with color filters in front of the lens. For instance, yellowish stains on a document can be eliminated or, at least, greatly subdued with a yellow filter in front of the lens. Since the document, as it appears through the camera lens, would then have a yellow cast overall, the stain would no longer stand out and would be much less likely to register on the film. Using a filter would of course lower the overall brightness of the document and necessitate a longer exposure.

Extra-fine-grain film that may be of limited spectral response is used in contact printers that make duplicate microfilms. Since the image has already been reduced to black and white, a film sensitive to all colors is no longer needed. The need is for a fine-grain film capable of high resolution.

However, the speed of a film, rather than its color response, is perhaps the most important factor in determining the resolution potential of a film stock. Relatively high-speed films are specified for use in rotary cameras where the exposure must be necessarily short as the document passes before the lens on a conveyor belt synchronized with a moving film. This requirement for speed of the film has the drawback of making the developed image more grainy—less capable of real sharpness or high resolution. But this usually does not matter, as the highest image quality is not necessary to make readable 16mm copies of letters, invoices, etc.

On the other hand, when engineering drawings or other physically large or very detailed documents are photographed on a planetary camera, the reduction ratio is likely to be greater, and there is likely to be a greater need to record detail. In such cases, a finer-grain film that is slower (requiring a longer exposure of the document) is specified. The document is stationary during filming, and the longer exposure is easy to arrange.

Manufacturers of microfilm cameras are, naturally, clearly aware of all this and supply or specify films for use with their

equipment. Well-known manufacturers of filmstock, such as Eastman Kodak, Du Pont, Dynacolor, General Aniline, Gavaert, and
a number of others, all produce films suitable for most microfilming needs. Generally speaking, the records manager in a company
without an experienced reproduction department will need the
aid of a camera manufacturer's technical representative or an experienced film technician if there is reason to believe that a film
stock other than that specified for use with his equipment will
improve the quality of his microfilm.

Microfilm, or any other silver photographic film, may seem at
a casual glance to be a homogeneous plastic strip, but it is actually
made up of a number of layers. In Fig. 11–1, strip number 1 is
probably the most common type of photographic film used in
microfilming. Layer *A* is the emulsion layer that contains the
light-sensitive silver halide crystals. Layer *B* is a thin binder layer
or "subbase" that helps the emulsion to adhere to the film base
through all the chemically active processing operations. Layer *C*
is the film base, a strip of acetate plastic that is flexible enough
and strong enough to be conveyed by rollers through all the steps
involved in photography and processing. Layer *D* is the "antihalation" undercoating that protects the film image from stray
light.

Films differ slightly in the approach to antihalation protection.
In strip number 2, the antihalation backing is contained in a dye
undercoat this is positioned right under the film emulsion. This
dye becomes transparent during processing, making possible a
projectable image. In strip 3, the antihalation protection is obtained by tinting the film base, thereby preventing stray light from
striking the emulsion from behind. In this case, the tint cannot
be washed away, and it may have some effect on the reproduction
characteristics of the microfilm when printed enlargements are
made if it is not compensated for.

Why is antihalation protection important? The reason is
shown in strip number 4: rays of light striking the emulsion would
pass through and be reflected back, either by the back of the film
or the back of the camera. The result would be light striking the
emulsion from behind and fogging the film—creating tiny halos
around elements of the image. That is why the type of film shown
in strip 4 would not be suited to normal photographic applications.

On first contact with microfilming, one is inclined to think of it exclusively in terms of the silver emulsion film discussed so far in this chapter. It is true that practically all original microfilms are photographed on silver emulsion film, but all duplicate films are not. Present-day requirements for clean and easy methods of

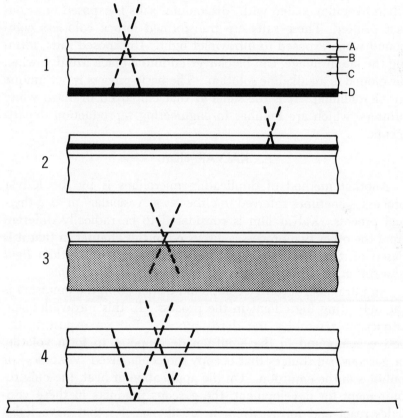

Fig. 11–1. Greatly magnified cross-section of various layers in film emulsions.

duplicating microfilm under office conditions have spurred the development of additional processes for this purpose. The reference here is to duplicating microfilms and not to the making of enlargements or hard-copy prints. There are frequent systems needs to duplicate rolls of microfilm in order to meet requirements that were not foreseen when the original order was placed with a microfilm service company or an in-plant microfilm department. Two additional processes are available that can be employed with equipment that is easy for clerical personnel to operate.

DIAZO FILM

One such equipment type makes use of the diazo process, whereby a film coated with "diazonium" salts is exposed in a contact printer. These salts are transformed into a colorless compound when exposed to ultraviolet light. Unexposed salts, forming the latent image, can be converted into a black azo dye when developed in an alkaline solution. The basic process is not unique to microfilming. It is the same as that employed in diazo white printers, which are familiar to engineering reproduction departments.

KALVAR FILM

Another method of duplicating microfilms is by the Kalvar process, sometimes referred to either as a "vesicular" or as a thermal process. Kalvar film is considered to be radically different from the other two processes discussed in this chapter in that it is based on the phenomenon of *light scattering* rather than *light absorption*, as occurs with silver emulsion and diazo films.

An ultraviolet sensitive compound dispersed in the emulsion is the activating ingredient in the process. In this ultraviolet sensitivity, it resembles the diazo process. But on exposure, the active compound in the emulsion decomposes to form volatile, or gaseous, substances that occupy molecular-sized "vesicules" or bubbles in the emulsion. On the application of heat, the only requirement for development, the gaseous products in these vesicules react and form extremely small particles that have light-refracting properties—the ability to scatter rather than transmit light.

In other words, instead of absorbing light, as do the silver emulsion or diazo dyes, the light-refracting elements scatter light and thereby block its transmission. The light-refracting elements of a Kalvar film can block the transmission of light through the background area of a film frame and allow it to pass through the area where the image is registered. This results in a negative film if a positive image is copied. However, Kalvar processes that provide a positive image from a positive film are more customarily used.

A distinction between the three types of film stock mentioned here is that silver film provides a reverse image, whereas the diazo and Kalvar processes can provide *direct-positive* images. This means that a silver film will always yield a negative image when a positive document is photographed or a positive film is copied. The other two processes, on the other hand, yield *direct positives*.

We all know that when we take a snapshot with a camera we get a negative before we get a positive. The same is true of silver microfilm, but it is not true of the diazo and Kalvar processes. They yield a positive from a positive, a considerable help in the design of microfilm duplicators for office use. Desk-top diazo and Kalvar aperture card copiers, such as those available from the 3M Company and IBM, provide a duplicate of the image on the original card that is not reversed. Also, they do this without the requirement of development in liquid baths ordinarily associated with development of silver film.

COLOR FILM

In addition to employing the microfilm stocks mentioned above, some records managers may have need for color microfilm. Color can be important, for instance, in the making of records of complicated electronic circuits where color-coded wiring is the principal apparent clue to the design, and also in the making of anatomical records for medical files. Most of the high-quality films used to make 35mm color motion pictures or color slide transparencies are adaptable to color microfilm needs. But it should be remembered that the complicated triple-layer emulsion used in color films places a limitation on resolution that is much greater than with fine-grain black-and-white film.

Chapter **12**

Protection and Storage
of Microfilm

For purposes of deciding on adequate storage conditions, microfilmed records can be divided into two categories: ordinary commercial records that are scheduled for destruction after a life of fifteen to twenty years, and "archival" records that are expected to survive for periods exceeding one hundred years. In this chapter, we will first discuss the preservation of relatively short-lived commercial records and then proceed to the somewhat more stringent requirements for preserving those that fit into the archival category.

PROTECTING ORDINARY COMMERCIAL RECORDS

Almost any area suited to the long-term storage of office supplies should prove adequate for the storage of microfilmed records that are scheduled for destruction after fifteen to twenty years. Microfilm is adversely affected by the same factors that lead to deterioration of such materials as photocopy paper and cellulose tape. Most heated and air-conditioned office buildings provide desirable storage conditions: humidity ranges between 40 and 50 per cent and temperature ranges between 50 and 75 degrees.

Microfilm records may seriously deteriorate over a period of a few years if stored in an area where temperature and humidity are uncontrolled. If, for example, humidity drops below 20 per cent or rises above 60 per cent for long periods, microfilm stock may become brittle, or cracks may appear in the emulsion coating that holds the image. The cracking is caused by the fact that the acetate film base and the emulsion do not expand at the same rate as a result of temperature and humidity changes. Also, high humidity can encourage the formation of mold that will react chemically with the emulsion coating and destroy the image.

Deposits of dust and dirt on the film will contain hard particles that can scratch the emulsion as it passes through a reader or printer. Storing microfilm in closed metal cabinets usually offers sufficient protection against dust in normal commercial applications.

There is an additional factor to consider in maintaining the chemical stability of microfilm that will be stored for medium to long periods (fifteen to thirty years). This is the presence of chemically active gases in the air. A common problem in business storage might arise from the presence of gases such as sulfur dioxide and hydrogen sulfide. Protection can be obtained by storing the microfilm in the paper cartons in which it was packed by the processing laboratory and then put in metal canisters with loose-fitting metal covers.

In cases where microfilmed records are referred to frequently, they are likely to get scratched or otherwise damaged in handling. It may be advisable to have the laboratory apply a special hard coating to such film at the time it is processed. When this lacquer coating dries, it is completely transparent and provides a hard, thin shield that is resistant to scratches and staining that may occur during handling and viewing.

If coated film is eventually scratched or stained, it can be put through a "rejuvenation" process that involves removal of the lacquer coating with solvents and recoating it with more lacquer. This treatment process is available from a number of companies that specialize in it. However, if a master copy of such microfilm is in good condition, it may be just as expedient to have duplicate copies made.

PROTECTING ARCHIVAL MICROFILM

We have now discussed adequate and economical storage and maintenance of commercial microfilm records designed for retention for relatively short periods. However, records managers find themselves concerned frequently with records of legal, historic, and other significance that must be preserved for a hundred years or more. Additional precautions need to be taken in both processing and storage of such archival film to insure that it will actually be readable at some date in the distant future.

A manager responsible for protecting archival microfilm records should make sure that the processing laboratory is aware that it is handling this type of record. The lab will then take pains to see that no developing chemicals such as residual hypo or residual silver salts remain on the developed film to react chemically with the emulsion over the years and fade the film image.

In applications involving long-term storage, more attention must be given to consistently maintaining proper ranges of temperature and humidity. Storage areas should be insulated to aid temperature control, and air conditioners will most likely be needed to maintain relative humidity between 40 and 50 per cent and temperature between 60 and 75 degrees at all times.

Temperatures in the lower part of the range favor preservation; but, if the temperature of the storage area is below the dew point of the air outside, notice should be given that microfilm should be allowed to warm inside its container before use. Otherwise, there will be condensation of moisture on the film.

FIRE HAZARDS

Protection from fire is another problem that must concern the records manager. Here he will run into some contradictions that arise from the nature of microfilm stock as compared to paper records: (1) The proper atmosphere for preservation of microfilm requires, if possible, free circulation of air. This means air-conditioning ducts that can be possible avenues for the spreading of fire. (2) Microfilm can be endangered by modern fire-resistant vaults constructed with a crystalline insulating material that generates interior steam when heated by fire. Microfilm containers that normally allow air to enter will also allow the passage of steam. This could soften and separate the thin emulsion from the film base, destroying the records.

An answer to the first problem is contained in an authoritative manual on microfilm preservation published by the Recordak Corporation that advises that the need for temperature and humidity control is likely to outweigh the possible fire hazard in the case of microfilm, provided underwriter-approved automatic fire-control dampers are installed in the ducts of fire resistant vaults in accordance with the recommendations of the National Fire Protection Association.

In cases where microfilm is stored in safes or vaults with steam-generating insulating material, it is advisable to seek the lesser of two evils and pack the microfilm in air-tight containers.

In archival storage vaults, air should be filtered to remove dust and potentially damaging gases. Gases that were mentioned earlier, hydrogen sulfide and sulfur dioxide, come frequently from coal gas, illuminating gas, and the reactions that take place in certain chemical plants. They are also present to a harmful degree in most industrial or urban areas. A manager responsible for setting up an archival storage room should consult a chemical engineer to ascertain to what degree such gases are present in the area and what can be done to purify the air.

Microfilm vaults should contain metal cabinets, preferably with adjustable shelves. Walls of the cabinets should have openings to facilitate the circulation of air through the cabinets. And, of course, microfilm should be protected from water damage that might occur through sprinkler discharge or flooding. Record vaults should have drains that will prevent the water level from rising. Also, cabinets should be raised about 6 inches off the floor as added insurance against water damage.

However, the best laid plans often go astray. Real security cannot be guaranteed for any record. A records manager who is serious about preserving records over a long period will want to store a duplicate set of "security copies" at another location remote from the primary archive. The ease of making duplicate rolls is an important advantage of microfilm.

GENERAL SUGGESTIONS

Roll microfilm is similar to motion picture film. Over the years, film distributors concerned with the protection of roughly handled motion picture film have developed a number of practices that cut down damage in use. These common-sense suggestions are brief and well worth the attention of any records manager who supervises the maintenance of frequently used roll microfilm records. Some of the most pertinent are as follows:

1. Be careful not to rewind film too loosely. This can result in warping, since moisture tends to evaporate from loosely wound reels.
2. Do not rewind film too tightly. This can cause abrasions, particularly if hard particles rub against the emulsion.
3. See that viewers and printers are clean. Regular use of a cloth or paper tissue on areas across which the film is transported will do much to eliminate hard particles that scratch film.
4. Handle film by its edges only. If feasible, wear clean cotton gloves when handling large amounts of film. This will protect it against oil stains from hands and fingers.
5. Periodically, check any splices in roll microfilm to make sure they are holding firm.

Appendix A

Microfilm and the Law

Forty-eight states and the federal government have now passed a *Uniform Photographic Copies of Business Records as Evidence Act*. These acts provide for the acceptance of certified microfilm copies of business records as primary evidence in courts of law and in legal proceedings. The only states that have not yet passed a Uniform Copies Act are Mississippi and West Virginia. It should be noted, however, that, even in these two states that have not yet enacted a Uniform Copies Act, microfilm has been accepted in courts of law as primary evidence in those instances in which the original copies of the records had been destroyed. There is no record of any court ever having refused to admit properly certified microfilmed records as primary evidence in the absence of the original documents. Section 1732 of Public Law 129 of the Eighty-second Congress, which established the acceptability in the federal courts of photographic copies of records made in the regular course of business, is reproduced as follows:

§ 1732. **Record made in regular course of business; photographic copies**

(a) In any court of the United States and in any court established by Act of Congress, any writing or record, whether in the form of an entry in a book or otherwise, made as a memorandum or record of any act, transaction, occurrence, or event, shall be admissible as evidence of such act, transaction, occurrence, or event, if made in regular course of any business, and if it was the regular course of such business to make such memorandum or record at the time of such act, transaction, occurrence, or event or within a reasonable time thereafter.

All other circumstances of the making of such writing or record, including lack of personal knowledge by the entrant or maker, may be shown to affect its weight, but such circumstances shall not affect its admissibility.

The term "business," as used in this section, includes business, profession, occupation, and calling of every kind.

(b) If any business, institution, member of a profession or calling, or any department or agency of government, in the regular course of business or activity has kept or recorded any memorandum, writing, entry, print, representation or combination thereof, of any act, transaction, occurrence, or event, and in the regular course of business has caused any or all of the same to be recorded, copied, or reproduced by any photographic, photostatic, microfilm, micro-card, miniature photographic, or other process which accurately reproduces or forms a durable medium for so reproducing the original, the original may be destroyed in the regular course of business unless its preservation is required by law. Such reproduction, when satisfactorily identified, is as admissible in evidence as the original itself in any judicial or administrative proceeding whether the original is in existence or not and an enlargement or facsimile of such reproduction is likewise admissible in evidence if the original reproduction is in existence and available for inspection under direction of court. The introduction of a reproduced record, enlargement, or facsimile does not preclude admission of the original. This subsection shall not be construed to exclude from evidence any document or copy thereof which is otherwise admissible under the rules of evidence. As amended Aug. 28, 1951, c. 351, §§ 1, 3, 65 Stat. 206; Aug. 30, 1961, Pub.L. 87-183, 75 Stat. 413.

Since these laws specifically state that *certified* microfilm is acceptable, you should be certain that an approved certification form is filmed as the last document on every roll of microfilmed business records. This form serves to authenticate all documents on the roll as true copies for legal and audit purposes. You should check with your company's legal staff or counsel to determine exactly what form or forms will be required in your particular operation. Figure A–1 is an example of one form of certification —that used by a large multidivisional manufacturing corporation.

It is important to remember that the Uniform Copies Act differentiates between actual microfilm and any enlargements or facsimiles made from it. In other words, the microfilm copy is considered the equivalent of the original, but reproductions made from this microfilm can only be acceptable as primary evidence if the microfilm itself is also available for inspection.

CERTIFICATE OF AUTHENTICITY

THIS IS TO CERTIFY that the microfilms appearing on this Film-File

Starting with _____ and

Ending with _____ are

accurate and complete reproductions of records of _____

_____ Division, delivered to the

undersigned by _____,

of _____, the legal custo-

dian of said records, who affirmed that such records were received

or made by said Division. Said records were microfilmed by the

undersigned in the regular course of business pursuant to estab-

lished company policy of said Corporation to maintain and pre-

serve such records through the storage of microfilm reproductions

thereof in protected locations.

It is further certified that the photographic processes used for

microfilming of the above records were accomplished in a manner

and on microfilm which meets with the requirements of the Na-

tional Bureau of Standards for permanent microphotographic

copy.

DATE PRODUCED (Month, day, year)	BY (Camera Operator)

PLACE (City and state)

Fig. A–1. An example of a certificate of authenticity.

Further support for the use of microfilm in the maintenance of legally acceptable business records is provided by the New York State Banking Law that states:

§ 256. Photographic reproduction of records

Any photograph, microphotograph or reproduction on film of any of the documents and records of a savings bank relating to the accounts of its depositors and the operation of its business, which such savings bank has caused to be made in the conduct of its business, shall be deemed to be the equivalent of the original thereof for all purposes, provided that the original of any such documents and records has been destroyed, that such photograph, microphotograph or reproduction on film shall be of durable material, and that the device used to reproduce such documents and records shall be one which accurately reproduced the original thereof in all details. (As amended L. 1959, c. 80, eff. March 17, 1959.)

Microfilm is almost invariably an acceptable legal record. But, for safety's sake, it is recommended that you check with your legal counsel on questionable details such as the wording of your certification form, and also let him review your entire microfilm program from a legal standpoint.

As a general rule, you can assume that microfilm copies would be legally acceptable in lieu of any record, providing that the original record itself would be admissible as evidence. The major exception to this rule is the General Ledger. Some State Taxation Departments have taken the stand that a company may not submit microfilm copies of its General Ledger in lieu of the original. Of course, this restriction applies to the situation in which a company routinely microfilms and then destroys its original General Ledger, keeping the microfilm copy for future use. In the event, however, that a General Ledger had been destroyed by fire, or misappropriated, etc., then any microfilm copy of the General Ledger that had been prepared solely for vital records protection purposes would most probably be acceptable in lieu of the original General Ledger.

You do incur some additional responsibility when you put your records on microfilm. In the event these records are called for examination by government agencies or courts of law, you may be required to either furnish a microfilm reader-printer for use by the persons examining your microfilm or to submit full-sized copies of records contained on a microfilm roll together with the roll itself for examination.

In addition, you will be faced with the problem of providing an additional copy of the requested microfilm roll for your own internal use. This situation can be easily provided for, however, by either preparing additional hard copies of the records by using a high-speed continuous printer or by preparing a duplicate of the requested microfilm roll.

RETENTION OF MICROFILM COPIES OF BUSINESS RECORDS

In those instances in which original records have been destroyed after microfilming, the same legal requirement governing the retention of records that would apply to the original records will apply to the microfilm copies. For example, if an arms and ammunition manufacturer decides to microfilm his files of gun registration cards (which the federal government requires he retain for a minimum of ten years) and then destroy the original gun registration cards, he would be required to retain the microfilm copies for the full ten-year period.

On the other hand, be especially alert to the possibility that microfilm copies of records may be indefinitely (and therefore permanently) retained by your company. Since microfilm occupies so little space, not much thought is given to its continued retention. It is especially important as a sound records management practice that firm retention periods be established for microfilm copies of business records, and that these retentions be faithfully adhered to. Remember, the fact that a record has been microfilmed does not change its retention period. There should be no discrepancy between the retention periods of a hard-copy record and any microfilm copies made from that hard copy.

Many companies have found it desirable to microfilm records having the same or similar retention periods on the same roll of film. Then they are not faced with the problem of either (1) retaining an entire microfilm roll to satisfy the retention requirements of a few records on that roll, or (2) of having to cut out segments of the microfilm roll containing records past their destruction dates, and then resplicing the remainder of the microfilm roll. Microfilming records of comparable retention periods together makes it possible to destroy the entire roll upon the conclusion of a common retention period.

Appendix B

Department of Defense
Microfilm Specifications

Records managers, particularly those whose province includes engineering drawings, have been told in recent years that microfilm records must conform to "DOD Specs"—or, to spell it out, Department of Defense Specifications. Of course, this demand is made only in the case of companies that do business with the military. Also, we are concerned here only with microfilming engineering drawings, not all the other varieties of business microfilm.

Conforming to DOD Specs may be considered just another vexing problem by many records managers, and an annoying one since microfilm records are usually processed by outside service companies. The records manager has no control over the work methods of these companies and probably has little knowledge of photographic technology.

But it is for exactly this reason that the DOD Specs can prove valuable. Their purpose is to insure that processed engineering microfilm will be of sufficiently good quality to meet the needs of the Department of Defense and all of its associated contractors and subcontractors. Adherence to these standards will be equally useful to the company where the microfilm originates.

Some of the areas covered by the DOD Specs are as follows:

1. Quality standards for silver halide, diazo, and thermal-developing types of film. These are the three types of microfilm now used in business.
2. Specifications for processing microfilm.
3. Specifications covering steps in the manufacture, coding, and positioning of the film image in the preparation of microfilm aperture cards.
4. The performance standards of various types of microfilm reproduction equipment.

The DOD Specs were drawn up because the research and procurement branches of the military forces encountered trouble as a result of a lack of standards concerning microfilm camera work, processing, and aperture card coding practices among private contractors.

It is important that information, when on microfilm, be usable in all branches of the defense effort, or by any government agency or contractor. It is easy to see why. For instance, the specifications relating to the preparation of aperture cards are particularly important. If the method of coding on such cards did not conform to agreed-upon standards, it would be just about impossible to mix cards originating from different sources and automatically sort and retrieve them.

Specifications on the quality of film that include tolerances for image density and sharpness of image can be of great value to the records manager, whether or not his microfilmed records will ever be used by the Department of Defense. When he tells a service bureau that results must conform to DOD Specs, the bureau personnel know exactly what he means and he knows what he should get in return. When he is dealing with records that do not need to meet these standards, he can so inform his processor and receive whatever price reduction is indicated by the less-strict requirements.

In the same way, Department of Defense Specifications relating to microfilm reproduction equipment such as roll-to-roll duplicators, card-to-card duplicators, and printers of blown-up images can also help the records manager who may be asked to specify equipment for his company.

New DOD Specs, related to many different phases of micro-filming, are issued and revised at frequent intervals and may be obtained through contracting officers at the particular government agency a company may be dealing with or directly through the Government Printing Office, Washington, D.C.

The areas that the DOD Specs take in are also being expanded. Specifications are being worked out for the making and reproduction of microfiche. It is impossible, therefore, to suggest any source book containing the complete Specs as a unit. However, the National Microfilm Association, Annapolis, Md., published a compilation in 1963, entitled *Engineering Data Microreproduction Standards and Specifications,* and frequently publishes up-to-date information on applications in its quarterly journal, *National Micro-News.*

Glossary

Like many other dynamic industries, the microfilm industry has developed a technical vocabulary of its own. Since a working knowledge of much of this vocabulary is needed to understand books and articles describing microfilm equipment and systems, the following glossary lists the common terms used.

Acetate Film Jackets. Clear sheets of acetate separated into storage chambers used for the storage of short strips of microfilm (also referred to as Film Jackets).

Alignment Target. A guideline (a piece of white tape, a paint mark, etc.) that has been placed upon a glass mask to permit rapid and accurate registration of copy on camera bed.

Aperture Card. A standard-size tabulating card into which a rectangular hole has been cut. A special adhesive is then applied around the cutout area and is used to hold a microfilm image securely in place. The aperture card may be key-punched to permit mechanical retrieval of the microfilm image.

Automatic Aperture Card Mounter. Equipment that automatically cuts and mounts microfilm in aperture cards.

Background. That portion of film or copy containing no information.

Bit. A binary digit that is part of the two-digit numbering system that is standard in automatic data processing. The photomemory systems such as FMA Filesearch make use of binary code.

Blueprint. A full-sized paper reproduction of a document (generally a drawing) that has a white image area on a blue background.

Camera Station. The location, either fixed or temporary, at which the actual microfilming of documents will be performed.

Card-to-Card Duplication. A process that will reproduce the image contained in an aperture card. Frequently, this term is also applied to the reproduction of a duplicate microfiche by the diazo process.

Certificate of Authenticity. A legal form that is filmed as the last document of a record series and authenticates all documents preceding it on the microfilm roll as true copies for legal and/or audit purposes.

Coding. A predetermined system for facilitating the location of desired microimages. Coding may take any number of forms, ranging from flash areas on roll microfilm to binary coding in photomemory systems.

Density. The degree of contrast between the image and non-image (background) area of a microimage. Easily measurable with a densitometer; density is generally expressed as a numerical equivalent.

Department of Defense Specifications (more commonly called "DOD Specs"). Standards developed by the Department of Defense concerning microfilm camera work as well as microfilm processing, coding, and reproduction. All contractors and subcontractors submitting microfilmed records to the federal government under the terms of their contracts must conform to these specifications.

Description. An indexing term that indicates something about a particular document (subject described, originator of document, etc.).

Diameters. The term that describes the number of times a document has been reduced or a microimage has been enlarged.

Diazo Film. A relatively slow film composed of azo dyes that, in the presence of strong light and ammonia vapors, is capable of creating an image. Diazo provides a positive image—black from black, white from white.

Document. Any form, report, photograph, drawing, correspondence, etc., received or generated by a company in the course of its business, that records or transmits information.

Dry Process Film. Film that is not developed by chemicals in solutions (e.g., diazo film).

Electrostatic Printer. A reproduction process that utilizes static electricity for the formation of images.

File. Any collection of documents arranged in a predetermined manner (numerically, randomly, chronologically, etc.).

Film Chips. Microfilm that has been cut into small sections (or chips).

Film Jackets. *See* Acetate Film Jackets.

Flash Card Indexing. A simple microfilm indexing system that subdivides the microfilm roll into smaller, easier searched segments by inserting blank spaces at predetermined intervals. These blank spaces, when viewed on a microfilm reader, appear as white flashes.

Frame. A single microfilm exposure.

Generation. A copy produced from an original microimage or a copy that has been created from that microimage. Thus, the original microfilm roll would be a first generation film, while a positive copy of that roll would be the second generation film, etc.

Generation Test. A means of determining the number of times usable copies may be reproduced from succeeding generations of microfilm. In this test, copies are successively reproduced until a print has been generated that is unusable. This indicates the anticipated range of copies that may be reasonably expected from that microfilm.

Hand Aperture Card Mounter. Equipment for cutting and mounting microfilm in aperture cards that must be manually operated.

Hard Copy. The original document or reproduced paper copy made from microfilm. It can also refer to a printout from such data processing media as magnetic tape or tabulating cards.

Hit. A term used to describe the matching of items in a file being mechanically searched.

Intermediate. A microfilm print that is intended to serve as the master for making successive prints or enlargements (microfiche, microfilm aperture cards, etc.).

Microcard. *See* Micro-Opaque Cards.

Microfiche. A unitized microform in which a group of related images is arranged on a transparent sheet of film in the same manner that dates appear on a calendar.

Microform. A generic term for any form, either film or paper, that contains microimages.

Micro-Opaque Cards. A unitized microform in which positive microimages are arranged on a white card in the manner in which dates appear on a calendar.

Microphotography. The production and utilization of miniaturized film copies of documents.

Microtape. A unitized microform in which an adhesive is applied to a positive paper print of roll microfilm and is subsequently cut to lengths and mounted on index card stock.

Negative Image. A photographic image in which the tonal values are reversed from the original, with whites appearing as black and blacks appearing as white.

Non-unitized Microfilm. Microforms that contain unrelated information units. Frequently, roll microfilm will be non-unitized, since it will contain a variety of unrelated information units on the same roll.

Planetary Camera. A camera in which the film unit is suspended over a flat copyboard. The documents are placed on the copyboard and are photographed while remaining motionless.

Positive Image. A photographic image in which the tonal values are identical with the original, with whites appearing as white, and blacks appearing as black.

Readers. Equipment capable of enlarging microimages to a size that can be read with the naked eye. The images are projected on a groundglass screen.

Reader-Printers. Equipment that in addition to enlarging microimages to readable size can also make paper copies of selected images.

Reduction Ratio. The ratio indicating the number of times the original document has been reduced while being microfilmed; e.g., a 16:1 reduction ratio would indicate that the original has been reduced to 1/16 of its original size.

Rejuvenation. A process that removes superficial scratches and stains on microfilm that has been coated with lacquer. This lacquer coating is removed with solvents and new lacquer is applied.

Resolution. The ability of a lens or photosensitive material to separate closely spaced information on a microimage. Resolution is expressed in lines per millimeter.

Rotary Camera. A camera in which the documents are transported by a moving belt before the film where they are photographed.

Silver Film. A film consisting of silver halide crystals coated with gelatin that releases free silver on exposure to light and developer.

Source Document. A document that provides information required for decision making or the further processing of data.

Step and Repeat. A photographic technique in which a group of documents is exposed in multiple rows upon a sheet of film. The camera automatically positions the images on the film.

Target. Markers filmed as part of a microfilm roll that are used to determine resolution, identify the documents being photographed, sectionalize the roll for easier reference, certify the documents photographed as true copies, etc.

Uniform Copies Act. The short title for the Uniform Photographic Copies of Business Records as Evidence Act. This act provides for the acceptance of certified microfilm copies of business records as primary evidence in courts of law and in legal proceedings.

Unitized. Refers to microforms that are planned as one complete unit or subdivision of information without reference or attachment to any unrelated or extraneous material (microfiche, aperture cards, etc.).

Index